chapman

chapman

3-D Wizardry

3-D Wizardry

Design in Papier-Mâché, Plaster and Foam

George Wolfe

Davis Publications, Inc.

Worcester, Massachusetts

*To all my loves — Catherine, David,
Michael, Philip and the fellers Barney and
Attila the Bun*

COPYRIGHT 1995

Davis Publications, Inc.
Worcester, Massachusetts U.S.A.

Cover art courtesy of Joe Barth, Barth
Brothers, New Orleans, Louisiana.
Photograph by Barry Barth.

Editor: Nancy Burnett
Design and Composition: Janis Owens

Library of Congress Catalog Card Number:
94-072580

ISBN: 0-87192-294-0

10 9 8 7 6 5 4 3 2

Acknowledgments

I wish to express my thanks to all the people who helped make this book possible. Most important are my wife, Catherine, for her patience and encouragement and my three sons, David, Michael and Philip, who participated in almost every part of the book.

Special appreciation goes to David Baker who discovered me and my dragons, and encouraged me to share my experiences with other art educators through *School Arts* Magazine. Along the way, I found kindred spirits in Bill Detmers of Culver-Stockton College, Rivers Murphy of Northwestern State University and Pierson Marshall of Isidore Newman School, all of whom provided support and technical advice.

The greatest experience in teaching is getting as much from my students as I give to them. Because this book is a legacy of shared ideas and creations I've collected for several years, I wish to thank the students who contributed to them: Chris Spurney, Roger Schneideau, Lee Lovejoy, Michael Wolfe, Lynell Brown, John Langlois, David Langlois, David Wolfe, David Indest, Philip Wolfe, Sammy Yoselevitz, Jimmy Cambias, Margaret Meyers, Matt Dollacker, James Johnson, Joey Darlak, Rachel Blackman, Vanessa D'Sousa, Craig Classen, Dominick Amato, Jenny Lewis, Sofia Strata, Lindsey York, Cambell Hutchison, Peyton Manning, Banks Griffin, Marc Koretsky, Lori Kushner, Beth Levy, Amy Wallace, Cameron Johnson, Steve Bellaire, Julian Morrison, Daniel Kern and countless others. I also want to thank the Administration, Board of Directors and alumni of Isidore Newman School, and especially Fine Arts Chairperson Karen Greenberg for allowing me to march to a different drummer.

Working behind the scenes are a whole group of talented artists-in-the-trade who design, decorate and build artwork for parades, balls, theater costumes, puppets and conventions. Most of their work goes unsigned and unacknowledged. For their help and sharing of trade techniques I want to spotlight sculptors Julian Strock and Mike Smith of Royal Artists, Henri Schindler of Comus, Russell Elliot, Luis Colmeneres, Jeff Cole, puppeteer Harry Mayronne, Jr., Tix Smith of Dallas Puppet Theater and, last but by no means least, designer/sculptors Joe Barth III and the entire Barth Brothers organization for their talent and assistance. Extra-special appreciation goes to the one man most of us haven't met, but who is hereby elected our mentor, Red Grooms.

Thanks also to Joan André for her costumes; Willa Shalit, Dean Ericson and Jayne Williams for life casting; Frank Gendusa for modeling; Jesselyn Zurik for her assemblages; Ida Kohlmeyer for becoming a sculptor; the Contemporary Art Center, New Orleans for originating the Krewe of Clones; and Lloyd Frischertz and the Krewe of Tucks, who sponsored the Dragons of New Orleans. While most of the drawings and photographs were made by the author, I must thank Fred Kahn and Sam Corenswet of Colorpix for the lab work. A big thank you goes to Mildred Covert for typing and spelling corrections.

I am also grateful to many collectors, including the Sidney Besthoff, K + B Plaza and Virlane Foundation, whose corporate collection is one of the finest in the South; the Historic New Orleans Collection; Charles Davis of the Davis Gallery of African Art in New Orleans; as well as the private collections of Mr. and Mrs. Romaldo Gonzalez, Catherine Wolfe, Ruth Mullen, Bill Lockhart and Betty Street. Special thanks go to Martha Siegel and Davis Publications' Nancy Burnett and Wyatt Wade for the opportunity to be seen and heard.

Contents

Contents

Contents

The Odyssey

An Introduction

This book is a tour of three-dimensional design and construction that can open a whole new world to students young and old. Beyond building small clay pieces, sculpture is often neglected in schools because materials such as stone, wood, metals and plastics are either too expensive, require sophisticated tools or are inappropriate for the age of the children. In addition, many teachers have little experience in three-dimensional work and sometimes need encouragement to expand their own horizons. Papier-mâché, plaster and foam fit the criteria needed to overcome these roadblocks. They are cheap, easy to use and provide media for all ages. Best of all they make large and larger-than-life works possible which, until now, were rarely found even in higher education.

Part Two contains chapters describing how to make masks, headpieces, creatures, puppets, human figures, constructions and assemblages in all three media. Chapter Eleven, "All the World's a Stage," illustrates the use of papier-mâché, plaster and foam in actual theater and school productions, as well as large community activities, festivals, installations, costumes and parades.

You may discover that, once you begin planning and building projects, you can't stop. You and your students will discover new materials and ideas as collective and individual imaginations grow. Art class is not only a place to make things, but is a workshop of challenging ideas where imagination and experimentation are more important than knowledge.

Enthusiasm for constructing objects in papier-mâché, plaster and foam is infectious in a way similar to the phenomena set forth in the movie *Field of Dreams*: "If you build it [they] will come." A simple idea or image can be a catalyst for change that can involve and affect a large number of people. "The Four Story Dragon," an activity described in Chapter Ten, was a solution to a need identified by school officials to improve a dull and depressing stairwell. Students participated in the project and kept the dream of the Four Story Dragon alive until it was finished. As a symbol of schoolwide imagination and involvement, the dragon is alive and growing. By allowing your students the freedom to think of and create wonderful works of art or full-blown theatrical productions, they will experience the joys of individuality and collaboration while contributing to the lasting joy of those around them.

3-D Wizardry

PART ONE

Materials of the Trade

Papier-mâché, plaster and foam have existed for a long time but have been neglected and overlooked as art media. While some might argue that these materials are not as permanent as stone, plastics and metals, we are reminded that neither are most two-dimensional artworks. No one has ordained that only forms created to withstand the outside elements are worthy of the name "sculpture." Recent art history has seen a shift away from this elitist attitude toward media. We find works in each of papier-mâché, plaster and foam that have withstood the test of time for their own sakes.

The great advantage of working in these three media is that they allow artists to experiment and understand our sculptural heritage. These materials are inexpensive and user friendly, providing many artists with the only opportunity they will have to work on life-size or even larger-than-life-size projects.

Papier-mâché, plaster and foam are versatile media for three-dimensional classroom experiences. They can be used equally well by students in elementary school, high school or college. Professional artists working in the communication and entertainment industries also use them to create such things as displays, stage props, costumes and animation figures.

While all three media are inexpensive, each has its own distinct characteristics. Papier-mâché is pliable but dries hard and firm. It can be either molded or applied in strips over an armature and can be waterproofed. Plaster can be carved, draped or coated on an armature or cast from a mold before drying rigid. Foam comes in two forms, one that is rigid and one that remains pliable.

Does your work need to be strong and durable, heavy- or lightweight, stable or flexible? Should it be waterproof or fireproof? Does it have to travel or be shipped? The choice of media will depend on your design and its purpose.

(Opposite) Architect Charles Moore, in conjunction with Perez, Ernst, Farnet, created this surrealistic fantasy design called *Wonderwall* for the New Orleans World's Fair (1984). He utilized papier-mâché, plaster and foam to divert the attention of passers-by from the reality of high tension wires and electric generators.

papier-mâché

Papier-Mâché Through the Ages

The French coined the phrase *papier-mâché*, or "mashed paper," but the technique of sculpting with papier-mâché has been practiced for centuries, first by the Chinese, then by the Persians and the Japanese. The most widespread use came during the eighteenth century in Europe. In 1765 Frederick the Great opened a papier-mâché factory in Berlin. During the nineteenth century, Victorian England revived the media with papier-mâché boxes, trays and even furniture. In early America, papier-mâché was a handcraft used for making utilitarian household objects before industrialization brought more durable materials such as wood, metal and plastic.

Today papier-mâché is often used as a basic sculpture media for children. Stage designers and carnival float makers are also among the major users.

Mexico has become a mecca for papier-mâché. Piñatas and numerous other festival objects, dolls and jewelry are highly developed art forms that rely on the medium. Oriental manufacturers of jewelry and keepsake boxes, among other things, have realized the importance of the medium as well, so papier-mâché still lives in the Far East.

(Above) An eight-foot rising sun shows the sculptural sophistication possible with papier-mâché. Courtesy The Mystic Krewe of Comus.

(Left) The dragon, in this case a highly complex papier-mâché sculpture, is a universal symbol of imagination. Courtesy The Mystic Krewe of Comus.

The Nature of the Material and Its Working Characteristics

Papier-mâché is the most versatile of the low-cost sculpture media. All the materials used are readily available and easy to handle. Projects can range from very simple works to complicated, sophisticated constructions.

Some apparently simple projects require complicated armatures. Making an armature, or frame, is a problem-solving event that can be a real challenge for the artist. The armature necessary for a piece might determine the age and skill required of a student artist.

There are a few disadvantages of papier-mâché which should be considered when selecting it as a classroom medium. Papier-mâché is not fireproof, nor is it very flexible, and it can only support limited weight. New adhesives and techniques have made it easier and faster to make papier-mâché pieces formerly possible only with an elaborate armature, but the sculpture process is still labor intensive, requiring a long attention span. For this reason papier-mâché is often done as a group project.

Classroom Organization

Papier-mâché requires a generous work area. Arrange your furniture to create a well-defined space fitting the needs and size of the project. Working outdoors is another possibility. Storage space for drying is important. Consider creating hanging space on a ceiling or wall.

Beware of making too much mess during one period of time. Sequence your papier-mâché classes throughout the year to help control space and storage needs.

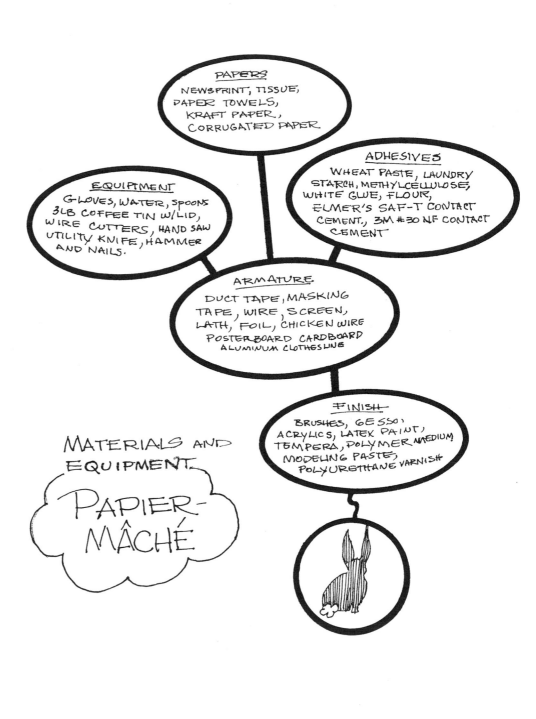

MATERIALS AND EQUIPMENT

PAPIER-MÂCHÉ

PAPERS
NEWSPRINT, TISSUE, PAPER TOWELS, KRAFT PAPER, CORRUGATED PAPER

ADHESIVES
WHEAT PASTE, LAUNDRY STARCH, METHYLCELLULOSE, WHITE GLUE, FLOUR, ELMER'S SAF-T CONTACT CEMENT, 3M #30 NF CONTACT CEMENT

EQUIPMENT
GLOVES, WATER, SPOONS 3LB COFFEE TIN W/LID, WIRE CUTTERS, HAND SAW UTILITY KNIFE, HAMMER AND NAILS.

ARMATURE
DUCT TAPE, MASKING TAPE, WIRE, SCREEN, LATH, FOIL, CHICKEN WIRE POSTERBOARD CARDBOARD ALUMINUM CLOTHESLINE

FINISH
BRUSHES, GESSO, ACRYLICS, LATEX PAINT, TEMPERA, POLYMER MEDIUM MODELING PASTE, POLYURETHANE VARNISH

Methods and Processes

How to Mix a Variety of Mâché Pastes

Flour, wheat paste, methylcellulose, laundry starch and white glue offer many options for making papier-mâché paste. Almost all are readily available and easy to use. Selection will depend on the age of the artist, cost, ease of clean-up, safety and availability at the time of use.

Flour can be mixed with water to make the simplest of pastes. Sifting the flour first will make mixing easier and reduce lumps. Flour is safe and readily available at grocery stores. However, a flour paste must be used quickly to avoid souring.

Wheat paste is the most widely used of the papier-mâché pastes and is easier to use than flour. To mix a batch of paste, half-fill a two-pound coffee can with water. Stir in one cup of wheat paste for every six cups of water. Continue stirring until all lumps are dissolved and the solution is the consistency of heavy cream. White glue can be added to a wheat paste solution or even used in lieu of wheat paste for a harder layer or water resistance. Plaster or ball clay can be added to the solution to make a sculpture's surface smoother. Adding sawdust to the solution will roughen it.

Wheat paste is inexpensive and is usually available at hardware and art supply stores. Most brands are labeled "Not for human consumption," so supervision of young children is important. Unlike paste made from flour, wheat paste can be stored for a few days. Careful cleanup is necessary to keep an orderly classroom.

Paste can also be made from **methylcellulose** by mixing the contents of a two-ounce package into a gallon of cold water. Stir for about two minutes, then let the mixture stand for fifteen minutes until it turns into a gel-like solution. Add water to thin the mixture if desired. Continue to add a little water occasionally to avoid thickening while you work. When sold as Ross Art Paste methylcellulose is labeled safe and nontoxic. It is more expensive than wheat paste, but isn't as messy. It dries without residue and becomes invisible to the casual observer.

Laundry starch from the grocery store is an old-time ingredient for mâché paste that is safe, inexpensive and easy to use. Mix one-third cup of laundry starch and one-half cup of cold water until smooth. Gradually add two quarts of boiling water, stirring constantly. Use the paste while it's warm, but not hot. Reheat occasionally for best results.

White glue mixed in equal parts with water forms a strong mâché paste. It works well as a finish coat because it adds strength and resists water when dry. White glue is nontoxic and can be found in grocery, drug and hardware stores. Be careful of clothing, however, if you choose a paste mixture of white glue and water. It is difficult to clean out of clothes when dry.

Methods

Traditionally there have been two methods of working in papier-mâché, known as the pulp method and the strip method. In recent times a third has been added, which is called the contact method.

Pulp Method

Pulp is really just chopped paper. When it is in a liquid state it is sometimes called mash or mush. It can either be purchased from an art supply store in a ready-mix form or made by shredding and soaking old newspapers into a mash. Local newspaper companies sometimes give away surplus

SOAK BLEND

STRAIN

SQUEEZE INTO BALLS

MIX WITH WHITE GLUE AS A BINDER

MASH

HOW TO MAKE —
HOME MADE PULP MÂCHÉ

ends of newsprint rolls to schools and community groups.

If you decide to make your own mash, begin by soaking the newsprint overnight in water to loosen the fibers, then shred the wet paper into a mash. Some people like to use a kitchen blender at this stage, creating a newsprint puree. Next drain the mash into a sieve, colander or screen, depending on the amount you are working with.

An alternative to using newsprint is substituting tissue paper for pulp. Tissue becomes fluffy when wet—almost like cotton candy—and can be used to shape large forms due to its fast drying time. Tissue has little strength, though, so strips of paper or fabric should cover the form. The number of layers of strips you build up will depend on the weight of the material you are using and the strength required.

To prepare the binder for your tissue paper or newsprint pulp, stir together equal parts of wheat paste and white glue and add water until the mixture is about

Mixing mash with white glue as a binder for homemade pulp mâché.

A college student adds mâché pulp to screen armature. Courtesy Northwestern State University, Louisiana.

the consistency of milk. Mix only the amount you need.

Knead the glue into the pulp until the pulp feels like damp clay. Then squeeze out excess moisture. This mâché clay is usually used on an armature or in casting because the slow drying time limits the thickness of the form to one-fourth inch. Even then, drying requires one or more weeks depending on thickness, humidity and moistness of the clay.

The main advantage to using a ready-to-mix pulp such as Celluclay is the shorter preparation time. The binder is already in the mix; just add water and knead.

Except for very small objects, all direct modeling of papier-mâché pulp requires an armature. Almost anything that establishes the general shape will serve, such as crushed aluminum foil or paper. A small head might begin with a Styrofoam ball or a light bulb. The pulp is applied almost as a skin, with noses, eyebrows and mouths modeled. Yarn, crushed paper or string can be added later for details.

A good rule for pulp mâché work is "the thinner the better" because of the long drying times required. A limit of one-fourth-inch thickness is standard. In the case of small objects, one-eighth-inch thickness might be more advantageous. Drying time can be accelerated with hair dryers, heaters or a warm oven.

The Strip Method

The strip method, or laminating, is the most widely used technique for working with papier-mâché. Newsprint, tissue or kraft paper are torn into strips one inch wide. The strips are dipped into a pail of paste, then wiped between the first finger and the edge of the container. This wiping returns excess paste to the pail while leaving just enough paste on the strip to do the job. Excess paste weakens strips, making them tear, and results in a sculpture that is exceedingly wet and slow to dry. Strips should be laid in a crisscross fashion for support. They should be applied in a single even layer over the sculpture's entire surface before progressing to the next layer.

Before tearing strips determine the grain of your paper. The standard newspaper sheet tears easily from top to bottom, producing uniform strips. Tabloid paper, on the other hand, tears from side to side. Attempts to tear against the grain result in irregular chunks.

Each of the three types of paper commonly used for papier-mâché offers distinctive qualities to a sculpture. Newsprint is highly absorbent, heavy and strong. Kraft paper is less absorbent than newsprint, but still provides reasonable strength and heaviness. Paper towels are the most absorbent of the three, but also the lightest and weakest.

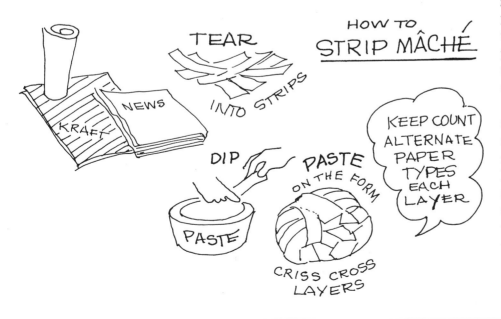

HOW TO STRIP MÂCHÉ

KRAFT NEWS TEAR INTO STRIPS

DIP PASTE

PASTE ON THE FORM

KEEP COUNT ALTERNATE PAPER TYPES EACH LAYER

CRISS CROSS LAYERS

It is a good idea to alternate types of paper in layers to give yourself better control and to help keep track of the number of layers you are building.

The Contact Method

Readily available contact adhesives have added options to the way papier-mâché is created today. When dry, the contact cement acts like pressure-sensitive paper that can be crumpled and built into a form by sticking to itself. Strips of kraft paper can then be stretched over the form, thus creating a skin. The main advantage of contact adhesive products is the drastic reduction in working time. In addition, these products offer the possibility of using lighter armatures for building sculptures that are lighter in weight overall. In many cases, a simple template of cardboard or thin plywood suffices as the armature. The most popular armature materials are cardboard, corrugated paper and kraft paper. Cardboard is most often used as a template (silhouette) of your form, but can also be

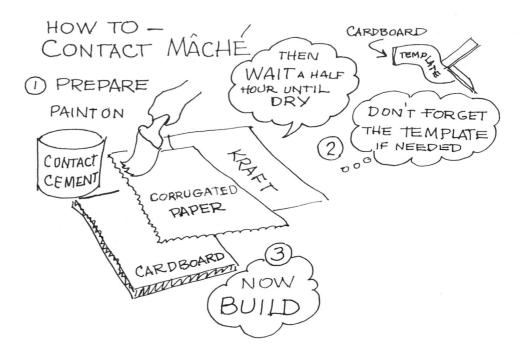

HOW TO —
CONTACT MÂCHÉ

① PREPARE PAINT ON

CONTACT CEMENT

CORRUGATED PAPER

KRAFT

CARDBOARD

THEN WAIT A HALF HOUR UNTIL DRY

CARDBOARD TEMPLATE

DON'T FORGET THE TEMPLATE IF NEEDED

②

③ NOW BUILD

(Below left) Contact mâché is easy to build with, and will stick to any cement-treated material when dry.

(Below middle) Make your form three-dimensional by slowly building up a shell of corrugated strips. Then switch to kraft paper to finish up.

(Below right) Contact mâché makes a sturdy base for strip mâché, which provides a smoother surface for finishing.

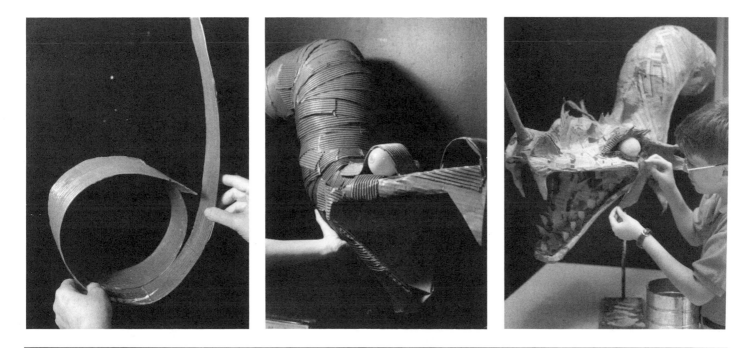

Four-Horned Creature with Friend, by artist Russell Elliot, began as a papier-mâché lift of a store-bought mask which grew and grew.

used in strips to build the structure in a way similar to siding a building in lumber. Or cut corrugated paper in strips and bend them to fill out the form. Then layer strips of kraft paper to build up the skin.

Adhesives for Contact Mâché

In this method of papier-mâché, all materials are coated with pressure-sensitive contact cement, which provides instant adhesion and allows the artist to build intuitively when the cement is dry. The main objection among students and teachers has been the messiness of traditional papier-mâché. As the potential of contact adhesives becomes more evident, papier-mâché should once again become popular in schools. These adhesives can only improve with time.

Elmer's SAF-T Contact Cement is a nontoxic water-soluble glue which is ready to bond in approximately twenty minutes. First cut paper into strips, then cover both surfaces of kraft or corrugated paper with adhesive. When dry the strips can be laminated to build up the form.

3M #30 NF (nonflammable) Contact Cement has a latex base and contains a solvent that aids in drying. It has become a favorite of commercial papier-mâché artists. The glue is ready to bond in thirty minutes but can often be left for a week or more and still fuse. This glue can be thinned with water and is nonflammable. Brushes are easily cleaned with water shortly after use.

• **SAFETY NOTE:** This adhesive can irritate eyes and skin. Wear goggles and disposable plastic gloves when handling it. It is not recommended for use by young children. Materials should be prepared in advance by an adult. Use only in a well-ventilated area or outdoors.

Molding and Casting

Positive Mold

Molding is the process of using one form to create another. The process can be as simple as layering strips or mash over an object that acts as a mold. The resulting cast, sometimes called a lift, can be removed when dry, enabling the original form to be used again for making many duplicates or to be returned to its original use. A mold can be almost any object or combination of objects, such as a plate, bowl, toy or clay sculpture. Combining a bowl and plate could become the positive mold for a basket or hat. Two bowls held together could be used to shape a round object. In cases where the cast is made over and around an object, you must cut the cast in half when dry, pull it off the mold and reattach the halves together.

Always use a separator on the surface of your mold so the papier-mâché will release from it when dry. Depending on the material used for the mold, the separator might be petroleum jelly, aluminum foil, plastic wrap, liquid soap or powder. Applying a layer of wet newsprint without glue for the first coat over the mold can also serve as a separator from successive layers containing wheat paste and white glue.

When using foil or plastic wrap as a separator, don't be surprised if they stick to the papier-mâché and become part of the work. Also don't worry about undercuts (convex shapes) that won't release naturally. Just cut them in half and repaste them together to complete the cast.

Constructing on an Armature

An armature is a framework created to support a sculpture. Constructing a sculpture on an armature requires ingenuity in both devising the armature and building up the piece. The character of your work can vary with the selection of armature.

Wire, cardboard, face masks, found objects, sculpted paper, crumpled foil or paper, balloons, rolled paper and Styrofoam are among the materials often used for papier-mâché armatures. Consider trying a mixed-media approach to armature making. For example, the basic shape could be chicken wire, with sculpted paper and foil added for details. Scored paper combined with rolled and crushed paper makes a successful armature for a small animal. Add cardboard and wire to an old baseball cap and you'll have the armature for a creative headpiece.

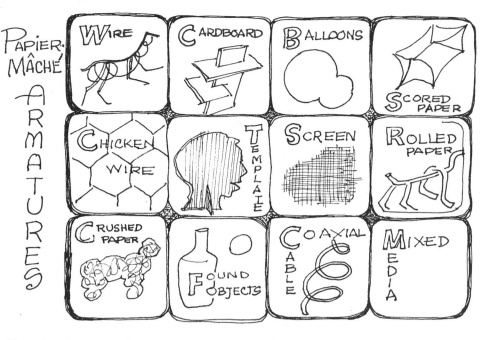

Examples of papier-mâché armatures for possible use.

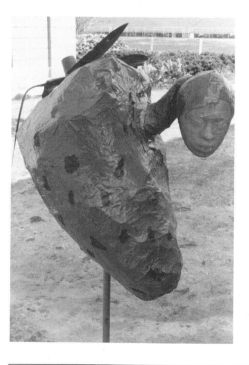

Eighth-grader Lynell Brown's *Strawberry and Me* provides a provocative insight into adolescence. Chicken wire, plaster gauze mask, papier-mâché.

plaster

Plaster through the Ages

Plaster is a very old medium derived from gypsum, a white mineral consisting of hydrous calcium sulfate. Plaster was originally considered a sketch medium for reduced scale models, but a surprising amount of plaster work in old churches and palaces has survived through time. It has been discovered in the great Egyptian pyramids. Ancient Greeks and Romans used it in their sculpture and architecture.

Heating gypsum produces the white powder substance we know as plaster. In the mid-eighteenth century, the French chemist Antoine Lavoisier developed a method of commercial production that spawned extensive use of plaster in the building trades. At about the same time, interior decoration had begun to emerge as a legitimate field in the arts in France, making frequent use of plaster, hence the name "plaster of Paris." Today there are many kinds of plaster but they all still come from gypsum. Fresco painting, painting on fresh plaster, can be found in many Greek and Roman buildings.

George Segal's *3 People on 4 Park Benches* transforms life casts into a powerful statement about modern life and the isolation of the individual. Virlane Foundation, New Orleans, Louisiana.

The Nature of the Material and Its Working Characteristics

Plaster can be carved from a block or cylinder, mixed with water and applied to a fabric, then draped on an armature, or cast from a mold. It is rigid when dry but brittle if dropped. While plaster is lighter than metal, stone and many woods, it is heavier than either papier-mâché or foam. One of its most valuable assets is its ability to capture fine detail.

Because it is relatively strong, inexpensive and easy to work with, plaster is an excellent material for schoolroom use. It comes in powder form that, after being mixed with water, can be molded, modeled or cast, or hardened for carving into sculpture. Plaster gauze is a plaster-impregnated cheesecloth which when wet makes a plaster cloth layer that can be laminated over an object to form a cast or an armature. Plaster takes a patina (finish) well and can easily be finished to simulate bronze, silver, gold, copper or gunmetal. On the other hand, plaster is messy. It produces a lot of dust that can get tracked throughout a school. A door mat at the classroom exit is essential to help control tracking.

• SAFETY NOTE: Students should use a face mask or respirator for any project in which dust is a by-product because of possible allergies. Also, skin may dry out slightly while working with plaster, so disposable plastic gloves should be worn to protect against dryness and avoid any sensitivities to the materials.

New methods of calcinating (heating) gypsum have produced a whole host of plasters with different qualities. Some plasters are soft and breakable, others are harder and more resilient. Some are better for molding, others are preferred when casting. Different combinations of plaster and acrylic, or plaster and concrete or acrylic and concrete have increased the versatility of plaster as an artist's medium. There are also a number of types of synthetic plaster available to the artist.

Materials and Equipment

Most materials needed for plaster sculpture can be found in grocery or hardware stores, or in stores that carry building, medical or industrial supplies. Knowing what materials are available and where to find them economically is important to both teacher and artist.

Experimentation with new materials and techniques, sometimes from unexpected places, is the only way to keep ahead in this field. The author recently watched a demonstration of life casting and realized how much the material used by the artist was similar to the substance used by a dentist for making a mold for a tooth crown. When asked about his material, the dentist replied that he used alginate, describing the different kinds available and pointing out a local source.

Classroom Organization

Special preparation and arrangement of furniture is important when using plaster in the classroom. Large tables are better than individual desks. It is important to have running water in proximity to the plaster mixing area. Dry plaster should be stored in a labeled garbage can or other container with a lid. Students should be grouped according to the process involved so that supplies can be shared and students doing similar projects can help one another.

MATERIALS AND EQUIPMENT

PLASTER

RAW MATERIALS
PLASTER, PLASTER GAUZE, ALGINATE, COTTON.

SAFETY
FACE MASK. DISPOSABLE PLASTIC GLOVES

ARMATURES
WIRE, SCREEN, LATH, FABRICS, FIBERGLASS, PIPE, FOUND OBJECTS, BALLOONS, WOOD, HAMMER, SAW, NAILS

MIXING
PLASTER, WATER, FLEXIBLE RUBBER BOWLS, OR PLASTIC BUCKETS, WAXED CONTAINER, OR MILK CARTON

SHAPING
KNIVES, WIRE BRUSH, SANDPAPER, WOOD RASP, PUTTY KNIFE

MOLDING / CASTING
SHIMS, STRING, PETROLEUM JELLY, SCREWDRIVER,

FINISHING
METALLIC POWDERS WHITE SHELLAC, ACRYLIC, OIL PAINT, TEMPERA. SHOE POLISH

Do not use a regular sink for plaster except to rinse off hands. Plaster dries quickly and will cause severe plumbing problems if allowed to dry in the pipes or the trap. A special plaster trap is used in orthopedic doctors' offices and in many sculpture classrooms. The trap, usually a removable container attached below the sink drain, allows hardened plaster to sink to the bottom while clearer water runs off through the drainage system. The trap is then removed for cleaning.

If a plaster trap is unavailable, use a large bucket of water for washing. Allow the plaster to settle in the bottom of the bucket, pour off the water and discard the solidified plaster in the trash.

HOMEMADE **SINK TRAP** FOR PLASTER

WATER

WASTE PLASTER

REMOVABLE CONTAINER TRAPS PLASTER

Storage

Generous shelf space is needed to hold works in progress. Molds alone can be large and cumbersome, even for relatively small finished pieces. Sculpture is three-dimensional by its nature, and that means lots of space is needed. Using a variety of

Materials

A variety of plaster and plaster-like products can be used for creating sculptures in the classroom.

Plasters and Concretes	Setting Time	Working Characteristics	Source
plaster of Paris	6–9 min.	lumpy when mixed, dries hard, breakable, easy to carve, excellent for molding for children	hardware store
#1 molding plaster	25–30 min.	used for molding, softer, not as strong, no additives, needs sealer, porous, easy to carve, breakable	building supply
#1 casting plaster	25–30 min.	used for casting, mixes easily, few lumps or bubbles, contains surface hardener/sealer, resists breaking, harder to carve	building supply
Hydrocal white or gray	25–30 min.	a gypsum cement used for general casting, dries harder and stronger than plaster, can produce fine detail, smooth, does not break	building supply
portland cement, white or gray	3 hrs.	a variety of cement used for outdoor sculpture	hardware store
latex/silicone liquid		liquid hardener for portland cement, used instead of water, stronger/ lighter, more weatherproof	building supply
Creastone		reusable cement, works like plaster, unbreakable when dry, becomes soft and workable again when re-wet	art supply store
plaster gauze		used to make positive cast, originally for medical use, strips of plaster/gauze activated by water, dries quickly and hard, almost unbreakable, minimizes mess	art supply store

storage methods is advisable, including wall hooks and overhead hangers.

Dry plaster should always be stored in a dry place in a closed container set on blocks to prevent moisture from seeping in. Plaster that has been exposed to moisture will crystallize and become lumpy. When this occurs discard it, because inferior quality will result. Don't forget: Unopened bags in storage must be kept elevated off the floor.

Cleanup

Leftover or dried plaster should be allowed to harden in a pliable mixing container such as a plastic bowl. When the plaster is completely dry, compress the sides of the container and the contents will fall out by itself. Any attempt to add water to soften the plaster will only make cleanup harder. The hardened plaster should then be discarded.

Before washing hands, scrape off excess plaster into a trash can, then rinse hands with running water. Remember: Do not allow lumps or sediment to collect in the drain. Spills on the floor should be cleaned up as soon as possible to prevent tracking plaster through the school.

How to Mix Plaster

Flexible rubber bowls are ideal, but plastic buckets or bowls are good substitute containers for mixing plaster powder with water because they can be flexed for clean up when the plaster has hardened. Rubber livestock feeding buckets are useful when large amounts of plaster are mixed.

Only prepare the amount of plaster that will be used immediately. Begin by filling a bowl to the desired level with water at room temperature. If the water

Mix plaster by sifting plaster powder with your hand until an island forms in the water bucket. Wait a few minutes, then slowly stir with your hand to break up lumps.

is too hot the plaster will set too fast, and if it is too cold it will set too slowly. Carefully sift the plaster powder with a sifter or through your fingers into the bowl, breaking up any lumps that form.

• SAFETY NOTE: Always wear disposable plastic gloves and a respirator or face mask when mixing plaster.

The proportion of plaster to water should be about two parts to one, or to the consistency that an island forms in the middle of the bucket. After a few minutes begin to stir the mixture slowly with your hand, breaking up lumps. Do not create air bubbles by whipping. If the mixture is too thick, add a little water. Plaster expands and gives off heat as it hardens, so don't be alarmed if you feel warmth.

Additives

Some additives can be used to speed up or slow down setting time of plaster. Others can be added to make plaster harder, rougher, fluffy or mottled. Still others can strengthen, expand or waterproof plaster. Plaster is generally best mixed at room temperature. A change in temperature will speed up or slow down the chemical action that causes hardening. Plaster sets fastest between 95° and 105°F. The chemical action slows down if temperatures exceed 105°F or are below room temperature. Intentional over-mixing (stirring plaster too much) can extend setting time while intentional under-mixing (not stirring enough) can hasten it. Adding salt also hastens it. In addition, hardening plaster can be accelerated by substituting a fifty/fifty solution of white glue and water for water alone in the plaster mix. Keep in mind that all hasteners or retarders can weaken the cast.

A whole host of materials can be added to plaster to change its texture. Materials such as fine or coarse sand, crushed rocks, cinders, glitter, stones, crushed glass or hemp can be added to the wet mixture or to the dry powder before mixing. All sorts of novelty materials, including rocks or glass pieces, can be glued on after the plaster has hardened. Modeling paste can be used to appliqué a variety of textures.

When baking soda is added to dry plaster before mixing a sponge-like bubbly texture is created. Vermiculite added to plaster and water roughens texture, making pieces lighter and easier to carve. The addition of vermiculite also produces a mottled gray color. Experiment with the proportion of vermiculite to plaster. Sawdust, perlite, marble chips, sand, zonolite, cat litter and even old coffee grounds can be added to create different effects. Try a three-to-one ratio at first, then try combining more than one material.

Troubleshooting

Symptom	Cause
weak cast	Bag of dry plaster exposed to moisture or improper mixing.
won't set	over-mixing, moisture in bag of plaster due to improper storage
lumps	moisture penetrated plaster bag in storage, or not broken up enough (under-mixed)
too many air bubbles	over-mixed
sets too fast	over-mixed, too much salt, or water temperature too warm
sets too slowly	water temperature too cold
soft and chalky mold	under-mixing

Methods and Processes

There are four different ways of working with plaster: carving, molding, casting and building up on an armature.

Carving

Find a container or other suitable object to serve as a mold for your sculpture's basic shape. Sketch your idea on paper first to help determine what basic shape to use. A box, sphere, cone or cylinder are good shapes to start with. Milk and orange juice cartons make excellent molds, as the wax coating acts as a separator between the mold and cast. Be a scavenger for waxed containers of all types for use as molds. Non-waxed containers need to be covered with a separating medium.

Use a utility knife or scissors as needed to cut the mold into the desired shape.

•SAFETY NOTE: Respect the tools you use, and always cut away from yourself. Use of sharp tools and cutting tools is not recommended for small children.

Mix your plaster and pour the liquid medium into your mold, letting the mixture run down the inside of the mold as you pour. Gently tap the mold to pop any air bubbles or pockets that may have formed. After the plaster is set, remove the mold to expose the block.

Make several drawings of your sculpture as if you were looking at each side of the finished work. Working from sketches helps you remember your plan as you carve and make adjustments on the block.

Rough in the general shapes first with a hand or hacksaw, or wood chisel, making sure that the form has an interesting shape when viewed from all sides. Use a wood rasp, hacksaw blade or gouge to refine the form, and a knife, scraper or sandpaper to add finishing details.

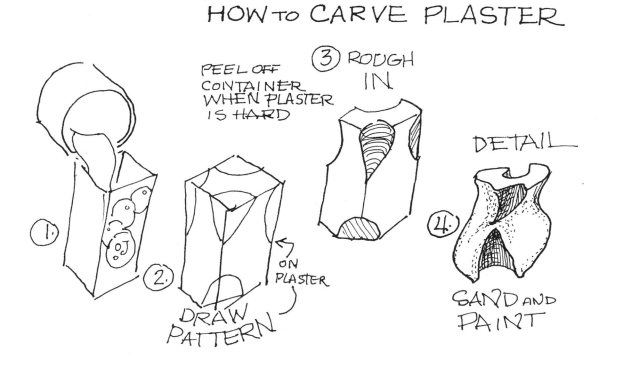

HOW TO CARVE PLASTER

PEEL OFF CONTAINER WHEN PLASTER IS HARD

③ ROUGH IN

DETAIL

①

②

ON PLASTER

DRAW PATTERN

④

SAND AND PAINT

Molding

Molding in plaster involves covering a model with plaster to create a negative image of that model. After the plaster dries the model is removed leaving an inside-out impression of the model.

One-piece molds are most often used for relief sculpture. Coins, medallions and cameos are good examples of objects made using relief molds. If the model is made of plasticene modeling clay, it is built on a base, with the image raised slightly to simulate three-dimensional space.

When creating a model for a one-piece mold, try to avoid undercuts so that the cast can easily be removed from the mold. If your model is a found object, a separator is needed to prevent sticking to the mold. Add bluing or tempera color to the first bowl of plaster so that you can identify the inside of the mold. Scoop plaster by hand onto the model, trying to cover it completely with the first coat. Succeeding coats can also be applied with plaster until the mold is about one and a half inches thick all over. Be careful to keep air bubbles to a minimum. Wear disposable plastic gloves for easy cleanup.

A piece mold is usually necessary for sculpture-in-the-round. This type of mold is made in two or more pieces so that the model can be removed from the cast and used again. Brass shims are used to divide the sculpture into sections free of undercuts. If brass shims are not available, you may use 1" x 2" strips cut from a manilla folder or other card stock. Placing the shims is a critical step in the success of a work. A "notch" or "key" should be included while shimming so that pieces can be put together in the correct manner.

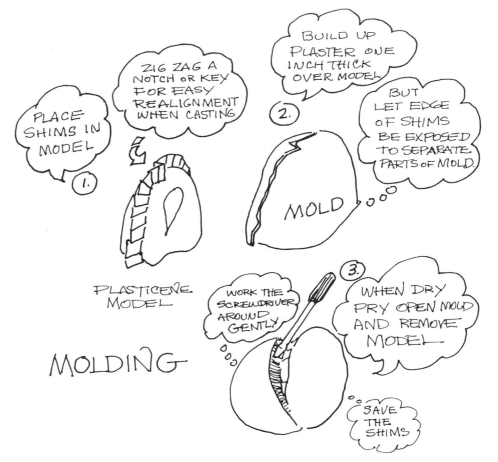

Molding plaster

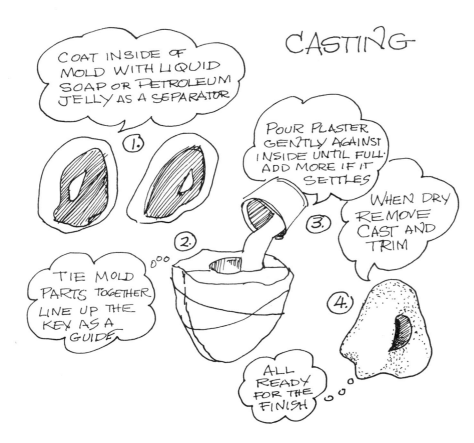

Casting plaster

Casting

Casting is the process of covering a positive mold with plaster gauze or filling a negative mold with plaster to produce a form. Molds must be coated with a separator such as liquid soap or petroleum jelly for easy removal of the forms, or casts.

If you are making a cast from a negative mold, pour plaster of a syrupy consistency slowly against the inside of the mold. Slosh the plaster into all of the mold's nooks and crannies and add more plaster until the mold is full. If you are making a cast from a positive mold, cover the mold with layers of plaster gauze in a crisscross fashion until the desired strength is attained. When it has dried, cut the cast to remove it from the mold. Reassemble the cast and repair the cut area with additional plaster gauze.

Building a Sculpture on an Armature

The armature serves as the support for a built-up sculpture. The armature may be constructed of any material that will work. The most common armatures for plaster are wire, wire screen, string, cardboard, lath, fabrics, balloons, found objects or combinations of these. Pipe or steel rods may be used in larger pieces.

The building up process is done by carefully adding wet plaster or plaster gauze to an armature and gradually building up the form until the desired shape is achieved. Burlap, muslin or fiberglass dipped in wet plaster can be used when more strength is needed. The length and width of the strips, and the number of layers required, will depend on the size and type of armature you use.

Dip 'N' Drape is a product similar to plaster gauze strips except that it is available in 30" x 40" sheets. Using sheets opens new possibilities. They can be draped over most armatures or used for folds and wrinkles in clothing and drapery. They can be knotted, flared, gathered, folded, tied, stretched, wrinkled, ruffled and plastered. A number of products similar to Dip 'N' Drape are available in heavier-weight materials for larger works.

Finishes

Plaster sculptures are usually finished with stains, paints or patinas.

Stains are diluted colors that can act as a tint on plaster. Dark shoe polish can be worked in, then buffed for a shaded effect.

Paints, either oil, acrylic or tempera mixed with a polymer medium, work well on plaster. Precise details can be painted on or an overall color antiqued with a darker glaze to add an Old World charm.

Patinas are simulated metallic finishes. Almost any metal can be simulated on plaster—bronze, brass, copper, silver—using a simple recipe.

Metallic powder is commonly used and is available in hardware or specialty paint stores. First dip your brush in white shellac, then dip it into dry metallic powder. Lift out some of the powder and brush it onto your piece. Lightly spread the powder on your piece making sure to cover the surface and all crevices. After the surface is well covered, allow it to dry. White shellac is alcohol based, which dries quickly, and the next coat will be oil-based or acrylic paint. The distinction between the two bases will prevent one from dissolving the other. Cover the entire area with flat black paint. Allow it to dry for half an hour, then cover it with talcum powder to hasten the drying process. Lightly buff the surface as it dries to rub away some of the black paint and to allow the metallic powder to show on the high surfaces. Work slowly, allowing the paint to dry enough to antique your piece. Some saturated talcum will cling to the crevices enhancing the effect. At this point you can either buff the piece and develop a low luster or apply brown liquid shoe polish as a tint and buff again and again.

foam

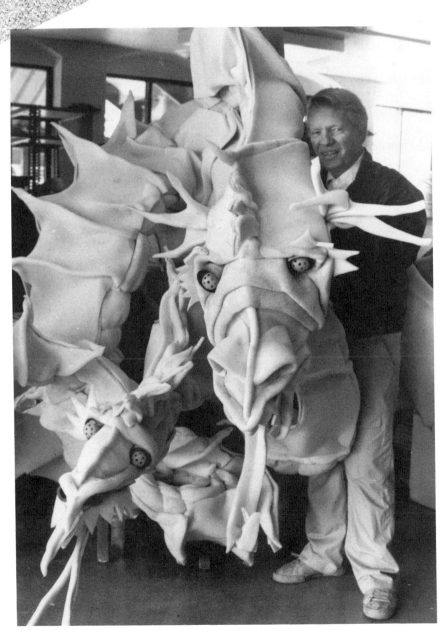

The Newcomer on the Sculpture Scene

The use of foam as an art medium is relatively new and still emerging. We are more familiar with foam as a part of our everyday lives. Urethane is commonly known as carpet padding. Styrofoam is found in cups, plates, insulation and the packaging of everything from televisions to computers.

In the art world, Styrofoam has been used for models in aluminum casting and for armatures in plaster work. It has been used to make puppets of all kinds, and theatrical and film technicians have used it to create entire worlds. With the technology now available, Styrofoam has become a medium itself.

Urethane foam seems like the infant in the foam family even though both types of foam are relatively young. It has recently begun to emerge as a medium for puppetry, technical theater, costumes, parades and displays.

Other types of foam materials are available, but Styrofoam and urethane foam are the two most useful as art media today.

A fantastic urethane foam dragon shows off the versatility of the medium.

(*Above*) Pioneering urethane foam artist Luis Colmenares and friend.

(*Right*) Audrey, the voracious plant from *Little Shop of Horrors*, demonstrates the creativity that theatrical and film technicians can explore through foam.

Gargoyles, griffins and other foam folk. Gifted and Talented Program, University of Southeastern Louisiana.

The Nature of the Material and Its Working Characteristics

Foam has great potential in school art programs. Both Styrofoam and urethane foam are inexpensive or very often free. Low cost is not the main reason for their importance, however. The nature of the materials opens new avenues of expression.

Urethane foam is soft, cellular, flexible and lightweight. It can be cut, folded, bent, tied, twisted, stuffed and glued into configurations not possible with other materials. Armatures for urethane sculptures often are made of materials which introduce another dimension to sculpture: movement. State-of-the-art adhesives are available which make intuitive design possible. The light weight and versatility of urethane foam make it easy to create larger-than-life pieces in a scale not possible in other media.

Styrofoam, on the other hand, is a firm, rigid but light material that can be easily cut, filed, sawed, gouged and pierced. By coating with a cement acrylic adhesive and acrylic topping, it can be used to create permanent outdoor works.

Styrofoam comes in a number of forms: blocks, sheets and throw-away packing material. We can improve our environment by turning discarded Styrofoam into art, making a solution out of a problem. Sheets can be laminated to make larger forms or glued together edge-to-surface to form geometric shapes. Blocks can be made or glued into solid forms.

Types of Foam and Where to Find Them

Urethane foam is available in sheets of three-eighths- or one half-inch thickness. It is commonly used as inexpensive carpet padding, sold in rolls six feet wide at wholesale carpet warehouses. It is also available at retail carpet stores by the yard.

Styrofoam is the trade name for a solid rigid foam made from polystyrene plastic. It is available in many sizes, thicknesses and densities. One-inch-thick lightweight insulation foam materials can be found at building material suppliers. Blocks of three-, six- or twelve-inch Styrofoam can be ordered through industrial supply sources (See Sources for Materials, p. 148), and molded Styrofoam shapes used for packing can be collected after use. Art suppliers also sell Styrofoam balls, cubes, cones, etc.

Classroom Organization

Generous space is needed when working with urethane foam. Large tables or open floor space is preferable during working time. Tables might be pushed back temporarily for extra space while work is in progress and returned to position for the next class. If this situation is not possible, a temporary move to the cafeteria, gym, stage or even outdoors might be considered. Cover the floor or ground with kraft paper and go to work.

Remember to clean up thoroughly. If working outdoors, do not leave scraps of foam to be pulverized by the lawnmower or you might have to live with them forever as tiny specks in the grass. Works in progress can be folded in a bundle and stored. Large pieces with armatures can be designed to be taken apart for storage.

STYROFOAM TOOLS AND MATERIALS

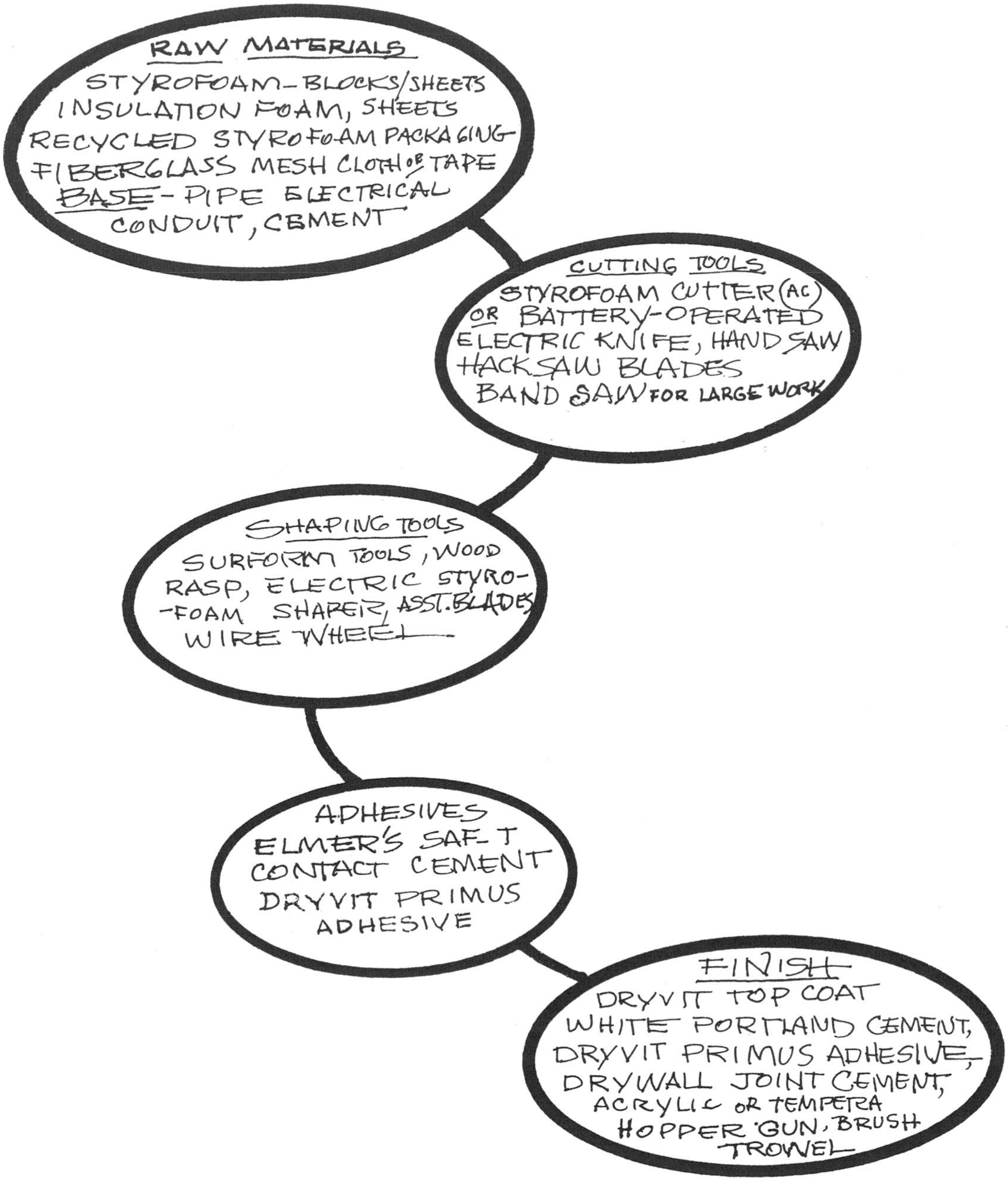

RAW MATERIALS
STYROFOAM — BLOCKS/SHEETS
INSULATION FOAM, SHEETS
RECYCLED STYROFOAM PACKAGING
FIBERGLASS MESH CLOTH OF TAPE
BASE — PIPE ELECTRICAL
CONDUIT, CEMENT

CUTTING TOOLS
STYROFOAM CUTTER (AC)
OR BATTERY-OPERATED
ELECTRIC KNIFE, HAND SAW
HACKSAW BLADES
BAND SAW FOR LARGE WORK

SHAPING TOOLS
SURFORM TOOLS, WOOD
RASP, ELECTRIC STYRO-
-FOAM SHAPER, ASST. BLADES
WIRE WHEEL

ADHESIVES
ELMER'S SAF-T
CONTACT CEMENT
DRYVIT PRIMUS
ADHESIVE

FINISH
DRYVIT TOP COAT
WHITE PORTLAND CEMENT,
DRYVIT PRIMUS ADHESIVE,
DRYWALL JOINT CEMENT,
ACRYLIC OR TEMPERA
HOPPER GUN, BRUSH
TROWEL

URETHANE FOAM TOOLS AND MATERIALS

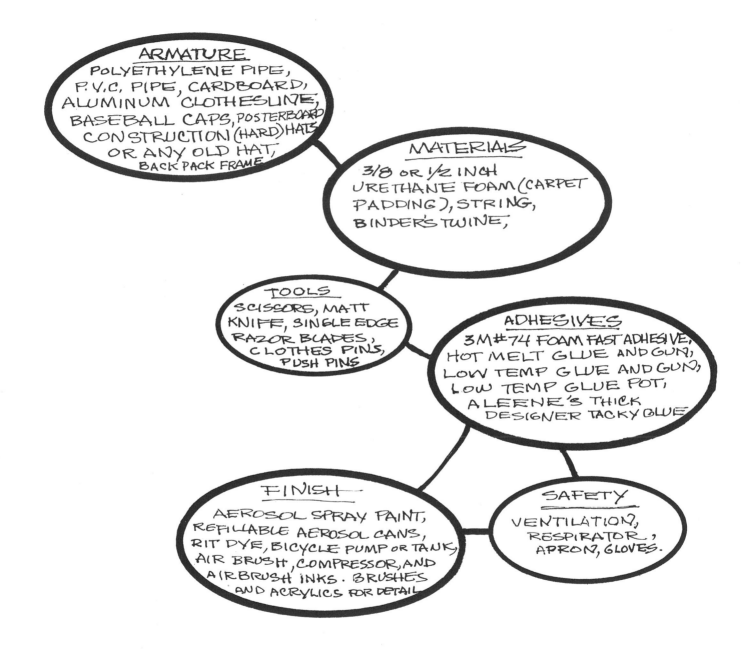

ARMATURE
POLYETHYLENE PIPE, P.V.C. PIPE, CARDBOARD, ALUMINUM CLOTHESLINE, BASEBALL CAPS, POSTERBOARD CONSTRUCTION (HARD) HATS OR ANY OLD HAT, BACK PACK FRAME

MATERIALS
3/8 OR 1/2 INCH URETHANE FOAM (CARPET PADDING), STRING, BINDER'S TWINE,

TOOLS
SCISSORS, MATT KNIFE, SINGLE EDGE RAZOR BLADES, CLOTHES PINS, PUSH PINS

ADHESIVES
3M #74 FOAM FAST ADHESIVE, HOT MELT GLUE AND GUN, LOW TEMP GLUE AND GUN, LOW TEMP GLUE POT, ALEENE'S THICK DESIGNER TACKY GLUE

FINISH
AEROSOL SPRAY PAINT, REFILLABLE AEROSOL CANS, RIT DYE, BICYCLE PUMP OR TANK, AIR BRUSH, COMPRESSOR, AND AIRBRUSH INKS. BRUSHES AND ACRYLICS FOR DETAIL

SAFETY
VENTILATION, RESPIRATOR, APRON, GLOVES.

Styrofoam does not need as much space for individual work projects. The size of Styrofoam projects determines the work and storage space required. Scheduling different size projects at the same time and directing team efforts can be useful for saving both time and space. Accommodations should include a place to use a Styrofoam cutter and outlets for that and other electrical tools. The Styrofoam cutter is a low-voltage wire cutter that cuts Styrofoam easily. A handheld cutter powered by a flashlight battery is also available at art supply stores.

•SAFETY NOTE: Styrofoam cutters are not recommended for use by young children, and should only be used in a well-ventilated area. Students using any electrical tools should be properly trained and supervised by the teacher at all times. Make sure that all tools are unplugged when not in use.

Cleanup

Surplus scraps of urethane foam should be stored for future use in a labeled garbage bag. All scraps are worth saving. Even the smallest can be used for such things as decorative details. Spray adhesive can be cleaned off with paint thinner, and hardened hot glue can be scraped up.

Cleanup is a bigger problem when using Styrofoam. Cutting, slicing, sawing, scraping, gouging and grinding leave countless tiny particles on the floor. A vacuum cleaner and dust pans should be at hand. Don't let Styrofoam particles get in sinks. If they do, you will have in effect a Styrofoam float valve in the trap. If this happens, clean out the sink trap.

A Few Notes About Urethane Foam Tools and Materials

Measuring. A yardstick is the best tool to measure urethane foam because the material is manufactured and sold by the yard. If your room has a tile floor it is probably divided into one-foot squares, which make a grid for measuring. If your floor is over thirty years old, it may have nine-inch squares; four of these equal a yard.

Cutting. If you're using a razor blade or mat knife to cut foam pull the blade toward you and cut with the point. Use a long stroke and let the cuts overlap when crossing each other.

•SAFETY NOTE: Put cardboard under foam when cutting so as not to dull the blade or ruin the surface of the table. Be careful to keep your body and other hand away from the blade. Scissors are safer for younger children.

Holding. Clothespins with springs make great clamps for holding work together after adhesive is applied. Small pieces can be tacked onto a wall or board while the adhesive dries. Cotton string and binder's twine are excellent tying materials. Cotton string is handy for more subtle knots and twists, while binder's twine is good for tying pieces together.

Adhesives for Urethane Foam

A challenge to working with urethane foam in the classroom is choosing the right adhesive to hold it together. The adhesive not only has to work and be practical, it has to be safe for children. The following is a list of adhesives and how to use them.

3M #74 Foam Fast Adhesive is a spray contact cement. Both surfaces to be glued must be covered. It tacks between ten and twenty-five seconds, after which it becomes too dry to tack. The spray head can be adjusted to discharge from a one-eighth-inch strip to a two-inch band area.

Hot Melt Glue, which is sold in hardware stores, makes a strong bond and is excellent for following a set pattern. It is not as effective for intuitive work.

Low Temp Glue performs similarly to hot glue, but it has a much lower melting point and hardens faster, so you must work quickly. It also requires a special gun. It is sold in craft and sewing centers. Make sure the name Low Temp is printed on each stick of glue and labeled on the gun.

•SAFETY NOTE: 3M #74 Foam Fast Adhesive contains solvent and should be used in a well-ventilated area. A respirator or face mask should be worn during use. Hot Melt Glue gets very hot and will burn if it comes into contact with skin. Likewise, the Low Temp Glue gun tip becomes hot and must be used with care. 3M #74 Foam Fast Adhesive and Hot Melt Glue are not recommended for use by small children. Middle school and junior high students should be supervised when using a Low Temp Glue gun.

An alternative to the gun is a low temp glue pot, a small electric melting pot for a low temp glue. The pot, which can be found at craft and sewing centers, allows three workers to work at a time. Apply glue to urethane with popsicle sticks. Supervision is recommended.

Aleene's Thick Designer Tacky Glue is nontoxic and bonds urethane foam well. Pieces must be held together with clothespins or tacked and to the wall with push pins while drying. This works well for masks, headpieces and smaller projects, and may be used by younger children.

Double-Stick Carpet Tape is safe and nontoxic and will adhere even to some complicated folds. The two-inch-wide indoor-outdoor type is preferable. The only problem with double-stick tape is the possibility of getting stuck yourself. Supervision is recommended for young children.

Urethane Foam: Methods and Processes

One of the assets of using urethane is that you can either systematically plan and build a piece, or you can experiment and work intuitively in search of an image—as an act of discovery. Of course you can always start out with a plan and use experimentation for the details.

A standard bulk roll of urethane foam, six feet wide by twenty yards long, can provide thirty-four thirty-six-inch squares of foam for individual projects. Cut out the six yards in the center of the roll, which will be heavily crumpled and lacking in strength, and reserve it for stuffing. Cut the remainder into the students' squares.

Pad the cutting surface with a piece of cardboard or other material to prevent dulling your blade or marring the work surface. A single-edge razor blade or a utility knife works equally well. Both can be found in hardware stores. Scissors are best for young children.

A wide variety of techniques can be used for making urethane foam sculptures. Many creatures can be made in a way similar to sewing. Two pieces of foam are glued together at the edges and then stuffed. Sometimes a template, or silhouette armature, can help contain one side while the other is being created, so that only one half is made at a time.

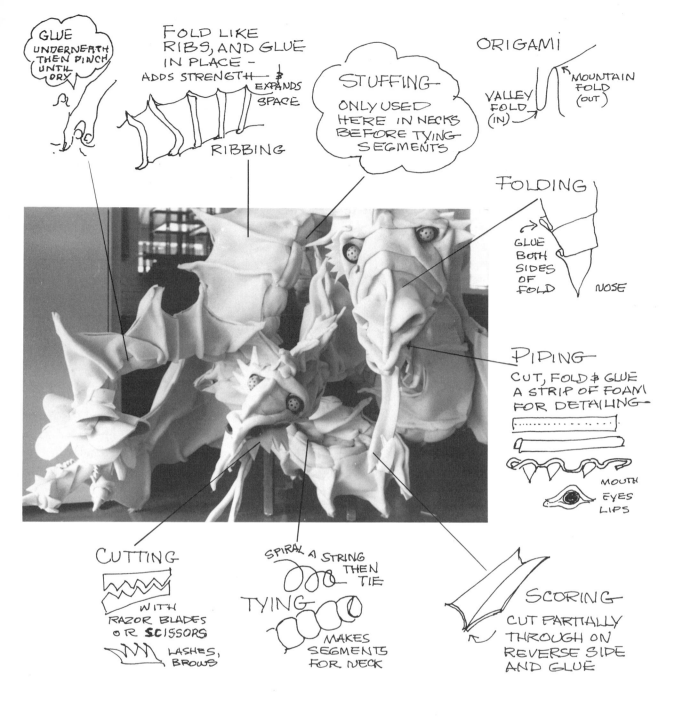

GLUE UNDERNEATH THEN PINCH UNTIL DRY

FOLD LIKE RIBS, AND GLUE IN PLACE — ADDS STRENGTH

EXPANDS SPACE

RIBBING

STUFFING — ONLY USED HERE IN NECKS BEFORE TYING SEGMENTS

ORIGAMI

VALLEY FOLD (IN)

MOUNTAIN FOLD (OUT)

FOLDING

GLUE BOTH SIDES OF FOLD

NOSE

PIPING

CUT, FOLD & GLUE A STRIP OF FOAM FOR DETAILING

MOUTH EYES LIPS

CUTTING

WITH RAZOR BLADES OR **SCISSORS**

LASHES, BROWS

SPIRAL A STRING THEN TIE

TYING

MAKES SEGMENTS FOR NECK

SCORING

CUT PARTIALLY THROUGH ON REVERSE SIDE AND GLUE

Methods and techniques for working with urethane foam.

Scraps can be stuffed inside sculptures to hold their shapes. A piece of foam can be pinched and glued or tacked for special effects. Almost any kind of twist you make can be fixed in place. A surface can be scored, or cut lightly, to enhance a fold.

The most popular techniques are folding and gluing. For example, creating ribs by gluing together rows of narrow folds makes a stronger surface, capable of supporting an expanded space without an armature. This technique, called ribbing, is reminiscent of the use of pointed arches and ribbed vaulting in Gothic cathedrals. Students may want to experiment with folding and gluing to devise new combinations of their own.

Another common method for holding foam in a desired position is to tie it with string or knot the foam itself, as in braiding or macramé. This can also add texture and character to a piece.

The paper-folding techniques of Japanese origami are almost a method in themselves when applied to urethane foam. The mountain-fold, valley-fold (which can be considered accordion fold) techniques are effective in creating many basic shapes without cutting. See Chapter Six, *The Headpiece,* or go to your local library for more information about origami.

Armatures

Urethane foam is so lightweight that new materials and techniques are needed for armatures. The lighter the armature the better. Posterboard, cardboard and foamboard can be cut and scored to create forms. Aluminum clothesline is an excellent armature for lightweight appendages. A whole variety of plastic pipe with different characteristics can be used for armature-building. Sometimes backpack frames are needed for mobility. Old hats and baseball caps are unusual supports for some creatures. Ribbing, stuffing and folding are some fabric techniques which can add support to the structure and extend the armature.

Finishing Techniques

An important step in any artwork is the finishing technique, supplying those extra details that complete a work and enhance its character. Finishing includes adding such things as features on a face, texture or color. This can be done by applying appropriately formed pieces of foam or other materials with interesting visual qualities. It can also be achieved by applying color to the surface.

The colors chosen for finishing should reflect a work's mood or intent. Is the figure calm and serene, fierce and grotesque or just plain real? These qualities should be enhanced by the work's colors. Some artists prefer not to paint urethane foam sculpture at all, but allow the sculptured quality of the foam speak for itself. However, foam sculpture created for puppetry, theater or parades is substantially more dramatic when painted.

You should not overestimate the ability of students to finish the wonderful forms they've created with the same quality. Color can destroy or deform a sculpture as easily as it can enhance it. Finishing must be planned. It's best to have a collection of photographs or slides from which students can brainstorm color schemes and techniques before attempting color.

Spraying is the preferred method of coloring urethane because of the foam's sponge-like quality. A wide variety of spray patterns is possible by changing spray distance, direction, speed and motion of the can. Spraying grazes the sculpture's surface with color, whereas painting with a brush will saturate it. Brushes are most useful for small detail work.

Paint

Acrylic paint is safe to use when mixed with polymer medium and water, but will not wash off with water when dry. Acrylic paints are sometimes sold in aerosol, quick-dry sprays. These are usually automobile acrylics (which contain solvents) and should not be confused with the polymer-based artists' colors. When applied to paper or wood the artists' colors dry fast. When applied to urethane they take longer to dry. A quick-drying alternative is spray enamel.

• SAFETY NOTE: Aerosol spray enamel contains a toxic solvent and must be used in a well-ventilated room or outdoors. It is not recommended for use by elementary school children. High school students should be closely supervised.

Equipment and Media

The airbrush is a good alternative to aerosol sprays and is useful for fine shading work. Jars can be attached to it if shading large areas is necessary. Another variation is the disposable power spray unit which attaches to a bottle for high pressure spraying.

Refillable aerosol spray cans are useful when working with a number of children. They can be filled with compressed air from a bicycle pump, air compressor or a portable compressed air tank. The refillable spray can works like a conventional aerosol can without the hazardous propellant. A number of refillable spray cans with different colors in each are more suit-able for classroom use (See Sources for Materials—Foam, p. 149).

Specially made inks are available for air brushes. These will work in any of the spraying devices, but can be expensive for large projects (See Sources for Materials—Finish, p. 149). Oil base paints also work well but need the addition of paint thinner (mineral spirits). Liquid acrylics are difficult to spray, unless an emulsifier is added to alter the viscosity of the paint. Instead, try using a refillable spray can and use the sprayer from the 3M #74 Foam Fast Adhesive spray can. This works extremely well. Or, use fabric dye (RIT) mixed with water in the refillable aerosol can. Just be careful not to spray clothing by accident!

Important: All alternatives to the aerosol spray enamel take much longer to dry. Sculptures should be hung up and labeled WET PAINT.

Color Scheme

Plan your color scheme carefully. Without a plan you can lose control and end up with a useless mess. After selecting a basic color scheme, experiment with your sprayer. Try different strokes for shading, blending, outlining, detailing, creating different patterns and simulating textures.

Spray lighter or brighter colors on your sculpture first. It is not necessary to cover all of the material. Shade and blend tones together with darker colors. Highlights are best treated with less paint, and more saturated paint should be used in the shadow areas. Paint in details last.

Try to echo the shape of and enhance your sculptured image. Be careful not to over-decorate. The sculptured form should have priority.

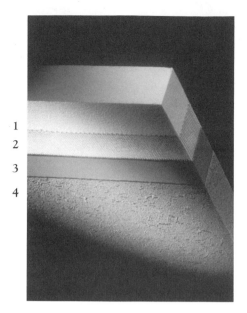

Think of Dryvit as a system of four parts:
1. the Styrofoam
2. fiberglass mesh
3. Primus Adhesive
4. Top Coat

Styrofoam: Methods and Processes

The nature of Styrofoam allows it to be approached like many other sculpture media. It can be carved or sculptured from a block, built up by cementing together planes and shapes or combined with pieces of existing objects as an assemblage. The essential difference and advantage Styrofoam offers is the ease of carving and assembling it. Ordinary home tools are all you need to get started.

A soldering iron with the tip replaced with a loop of #10 copper wire makes a great scoop. You can also buy a Styrofoam cutter at an art supply store or make one using a transformer from a doorbell to reduce the electric current to a safe level with enough resistance to cut the foam. An inexpensive battery-operated hand-held wire cutter is available from art suppliers. Large blocks of Styrofoam need more formidable tools like a bandsaw to reduce to a workable size.

• SAFETY NOTE: Students using electrical and power tools should be properly supervised at all times. Tools should be unplugged when not in use. Young children should be restricted from using these tools altogether.

The difference between Styrofoam and urethane foam is that with Styrofoam you do not have to learn new techniques or ways of working. All of the projects described here are reminiscent of forms and techniques used throughout the history of art, except that the Styrofoam works are lightweight and can be made almost indestructible. While most sculpture is designed to stay in place, lightweight Styrofoam can and probably should be designed to be moved.

You can carve Styrofoam very much like you would wood or stone. If you are working with a block or cylinder of Styrofoam, draw each view of your design on each side. Then rough in your shape by making selected cuts with a saw or Styrofoam cutter. Refine the shape with an electric knife, a serrated paring knife or Stanley Surform tools (available as a plane, rasp or round file). Often a simple hacksaw blade is the most useful tool for cutting and shaping. An electric drill with a wire wheel really grinds away the shape quickly, but disposal of the millions of tiny bubbles of foam may pose a problem.

Sheets of insulation foam are simple to cut and provide an inexpensive easy-to-work resource for the sculptor who likes to build constructions. Elmer's SAF-T Contact Cement binds well, but must dry before you put the coated pieces of foam together. Discarded Styrofoam packaging materials from TV's, VCR's and other appliances are a treasure for artists who like to select, arrange and rearrange their forms. With careful planning, many of these pieces can be used to create relief or round sculptures. Foam peanuts, whether combined with Elmer's SAF-T Contact Cement or used alone, are a fun variation for building sculpture.

The lightweight quality of Styrofoam calls for consideration of how to anchor a work to keep it in place. For the most part, the mass of a Styrofoam sculpture creates its own armature, but an anchor must be designed separately.

Styrofoam and the Dryvit System

Architects have been using Styrofoam for building exteriors and sculptural effects for many years thanks to an acrylic cement product called Dryvit, which provides a hard, weather-resistant surface. Dryvit's strength and versatility can also help turn

Styrofoam into its own sculpture medium for large outdoor works. Dryvit is especially useful for older students who like working with unusual materials. It is not appropriate for young children.

The Dryvit system includes three parts: Primus Adhesive, fiberglass mesh fabric and an acrylic topping called Top Coat. Primus Adhesive is mixed fifty-fifty with white portland cement to create a bond for the fiberglass mesh fabric, which is laid over the sculpture form and troweled with the adhesive. When this is dry, Top Coat is applied as a finish.

Top Coat is available in a number of different textures and colors. You can create additional textures by using different trowels, scrapers and brushes. Top Coat can also be sprayed with a hopper gun (a funnel-like dispenser attached to an air compressor) for a rough texture. Color can be selected from the manufacturer's selection, or you may add acrylic paint to make your own finish.

(Right) The Guinea, the Dancer, and the Column by Rivers Murphy. The form reflects its architectural surroundings with cantilevered planes balanced on a pier.

(Right, above) Each part of this sculpture was fabricated by Louisiana artist Rivers Murphy, then glued together with Elmer's SAF-T Contact Cement. A fiberglass mesh imbedded into an acrylic cement adhesive covers the whole surface. White Dryvit Top Coat was applied one-sixteenth-inch thick first to one area with a trowel (smooth) then to another, blown with a hoppergun (rough).

(Right) The artist has solved the problem of how to anchor his sculpture with a square pipe fit into the foam and a platform.

steps for designing and planning sculpture

The Design Concept

A well-planned design concept is essential to creating a successful project. The design process includes a series of steps to develop the concept: brainstorming, conceptual exercises, research, sketching and making connections.

The purpose of brainstorming is to list as many ideas as you can. Brainstorming in the classroom takes advantage of group dynamics and can generate far more ideas than individual brainstorming can. Don't try to be organized or practical. Go on a scavenger hunt for ideas. Make a long list, read it over and add details.

Warming up with some related conceptual exercises, such as sketching or constructing small paper models, can help trigger the imagination. These are visual-tactile experiences, which can later be developed into more tangible forms. For example, contour drawing can help you "see" and "feel" the contour of a model.

Gesture drawing is a way to understand and develop a figure's poses or action. Wire sketch studies are preliminary to building wire armatures.

Practicing paper scoring and learning paper sculpture techniques such as origami can be helpful in conceptualizing urethane foam sculptures. Learn methods of making geometric shapes from paper. Make doodles to search for ideas. Clay sketches can help you develop a form. Kinesthetic movement exercises are especially useful as warm-ups for planning armatures of moving sculpture. These dance movements help the artist conceptualize the movement intended for the sculpture.

In the research phase of the design process, review as many examples of other artists' works as possible. Visit galleries and museums. Look for pictures of artworks in books and magazines. Look at past as well as contemporary solutions. The observation and study of nature can lead to your own discoveries.

Developing a picture file is also helpful. It can be a source of inspiration as well as a source of examples of how real people, animals and objects look in different poses for use when you are trying to recreate them in a sculpture. Look over all of the steps for developing your concept and try to connect ones that make sense. Making connections should be the most creative step of all. Continue to review steps as you progress. Then narrow down your ideas and work for conclusions. If successful this should produce your *design concept*—a plan for your artwork and a summation of all that you have done through brainstorming, conceptual exercises, research and making connections. The next step is the building stage, which entails the selection and construction of an armature.

Styles

Style refers to the way an idea is portrayed and how it is viewed by an audience. Often the purpose of the work will suggest an appropriate style. Most sculpture is made in one of four basic styles: real, imaginary, exaggerated or stylized. There is some overlap and even mixing of styles depending upon a sculpture's purpose.

Real. The overall character of the work is loosely based on reality within the limits of that medium. For example, when creating a sculpture of a dog, the artist will make the work look as much like a real dog as possible, fashioning whiskers, ears and other features.

As we know from history, real can mean copying nature, as in naturalism, or the inner spirit, as in such realism as that of Camille Corot, or as in the critical reality of an artist like Honoré Daumier.

Imaginary. This is the opposite of real, with images conceived by the mind rather than the senses. While real objects are often used as the inspiration, the context, scale or space will change the meaning. Imaginary works are frequently described with such words as fanciful, visionary, whimsical or fantastic. The works tend to show a range of ideas.

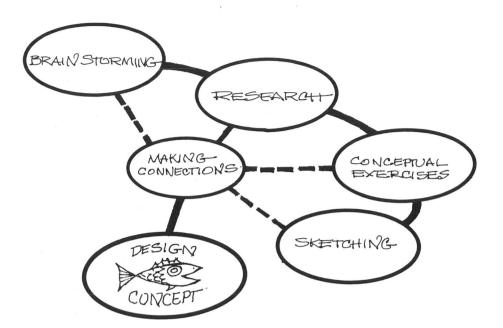

Steps for the design concept.

Exaggerated. The form is still based on reality, but it is changed to heighten some aspect of reality for artistic purposes. Exaggeration can vary from a relatively minor change of the scale of a subject's parts to a grotesquely altered characterization.

Stylized. The form is abstracted from reality into a convention or stylistic pattern. The Egyptian eye is an example of convention, or symbolism. The Art Nouveau period at the turn of the century, as well as the Art Deco and Art Moderne periods of the 1920s and 1930s, produced examples of stylistic artwork.

The combination of an artist's design concept and style will result in an artwork that reflects that artist's unique vision.

The Armature

The armature is the backbone of a piece of sculpture. Since it will determine the final character of the work, as much care should be taken in designing the armature and selecting appropriate materials as is given to planning the sculptural form.

Almost anything can become an armature for some kind of sculpture. Brainstorming a few possibilities for papier-mâché, plaster and foam, an artist might choose from rolls or wads of paper or rags, metal, wood, foil, wire, wire screen, metal lath, cardboard, sculpted paper, clay, balloons, fabrics, plastic pipe, coaxial cable, hats and other found objects, eyeglasses and a backpack frame. More than one armature medium can be used together to suit the needs of a project. As new materials are developed, the possibilities and challenges become endless.

A sheet of stiff paper or poster board can easily be scored by scratching one side and using the resulting score line to bend the paper and form a strong edge. Practice scoring on different geometric shapes before making your armature.

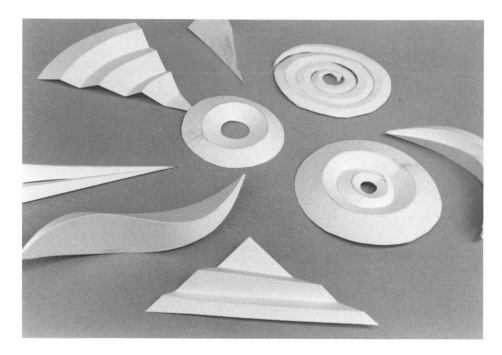

An Annotated List of Armature Materials

Wire is a universal armature material for almost all media. Thin wire can be used as a gesture sketch in small figurative work. Aluminum clothesline is flexible yet strong enough for figure work as well as for abstract and bimorphic shapes. Wire can also be used in combination with other materials to create an armature.

Corrugated cardboard sheets or recycled boxes, corrugated paper, tag board and poster board can all be cut or scored to make lightweight but sturdy armatures. Urethane foam can become its own armature by folding and gluing ribs (See Chapter Three, *Urethane Foam*).

Sculpted paper can produce excellent armatures for plaster, papier-mâché and foam sculptures. Scoring paper or poster board gives an opportunity to use unusual geometric shapes and develop form. The scored edge is much stronger than the sheet of paper, just as paper is stronger across the grain than with it. Pieces of paper or poster board can be notched and fitted together. Newspaper can be crumpled and taped in place to round out sharp edges or fill in gaps.

Cardboard is much more versatile for creating armatures than most people realize and can be used in a number of different ways for papier-mâché, plaster and foam sculpture. These techniques include cutting and scoring, creating slotted cardboard armatures, making templates for stuffing or building, taping and gluing to rough in larger shapes, and combinations of two or more of the above methods.

The cutting-and-scoring technique is similar to paper sculpture except that cardboard is more rigid. Most animal forms can be built with this technique. Geometric shapes can be constructed

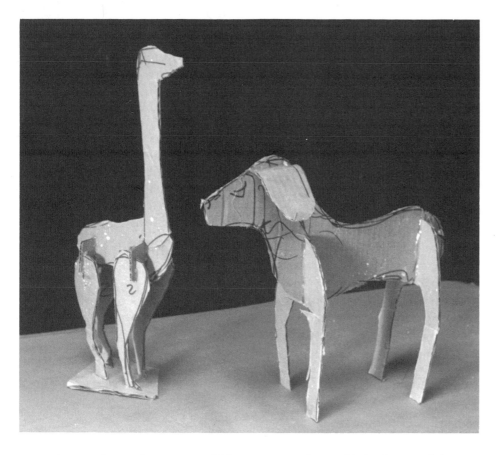

Slotted cardboard works well for most animals. It is often used as a mannequin in clothing stores.

using the simplest techniques available. Texture and relief can be emphasized by using ready-made objects as part of the armature. Egg cartons, fruit dividers and corners of boxes are a few examples of ready-made objects that can be used.

The slotting technique is often used as a sculptural form itself in wood and metal. Slotted cardboard is a particularly good way to build an armature for a large piece in papier-mâché or urethane foam.

This very simple method is often overlooked by sculptors as being too childlike or simplistic, but as you begin to use it you may conclude that simpler is often better. A number of creatures have been constructed to illustrate how little technical skill is necessary. Basic shapes are all that you need to develop form.

The use of a cardboard template as an armature for sculpture is a recent innova-

tion made possible by the use of the new technology in adhesives and contact papier-mâché.

Balloons are armatures of choice for spheres and bimorphic shapes. Balloons come in different shapes and sizes, some round, some long, some segmented. They can be joined together by coating the balloons with Elmer's SAF-T Contact Cement, then applying cement-coated strips to hold them together. They are also easily combined with other techniques. The artist that likes to conceive of forms as geometric designs will find a useful tool in balloons. Either strip papier-mâché or plaster surgical gauze can be used with balloon armatures. The balloon is popped and removed after a cast is made.

Found objects are used with papier-mâché and plaster as positive molds for duplication. Examples of found objects

---

might include seashells, drinking straws, buttons, plastic containers and sunglasses.

The human body can be used as a temporary armature. A liberal coating of petroleum jelly or liquid soap must be applied to a model's skin or hair before casting begins. Once the cast is removed from the model, it may be necessary to add a permanent armature of other materials to reinforce and support the piece.

Simple shapes such as fruits and vegetables—eggplant, apples, oranges and peppers—are easily built over crumpled foil or paper. Crumpled paper can also be used to stuff and build up forms for papier-mâché. Wads of paper taped together can be used to form general shapes or used in connection with wire armatures for animals and figures.

Rolled newspaper or cardboard tubes can be used to make the body and legs of an animal. Tubes can be taped tightly to each other or to other parts of the sculpture to form unusual shapes.

Metal and wood are often used to build structures or armatures in larger works. Pieces can be lightly glued or tied together with wire, thread or twine. Wood also makes a good base for many sculptures.

Cut bamboo strips that have been soaked in hot water can be easily bent into armatures for traditional Mexican piñatas. Old window blinds are also a good source for these strips.

Chicken wire armatures are easy to make with simple tools. They are most often used for big shapes. The large-hole wire is very flexible and particularly easy to use. It can be pushed into shape or stretched for thinner forms. It comes in one-, two-, three- and four-foot widths. The three-foot length is useful for full-size figures because it easily fits body divisions.

• SAFETY NOTE: Use protective gloves and long-sleeve shirts when cutting chicken wire. Tin snips are long-handled and dull, and work great for this task.

Various kinds of plastic pipe are available as armatures for lightweight sculpture. PVC (polyvinyl chloride) pipe is rigid and strong and can be tied together for stability of construction. It is available in hardware stores. CPVC (hot-water pipe) is smaller in diameter and although rigid is bowed more easily. Polyethylene water pipe is a semirigid pipe that comes in three-foot-diameter rolls and has the advantage of being formed in a curve, a shape it tends to retain. It is more resilient than PVC or CPVC pipe and can be used where movement is intended, flexing and whipping to create an animated quality. Polyethylene pipe is found in plumbing supply houses (It is used to bring water from the water main to your meter.). Polybutylene pipe is even more flexible but doesn't have as much strength. It is found in hardware or plumbing supply stores.

Plastic pipes are most useful as armatures for urethane foam where the main purpose is a base or backbone. Besides being lightweight and easy to use, plastic pipe is versatile. It can be stable or mobile. Many mobile sculptures are rigged on backpack frames, which can be strapped to a chair as a base or unbuckled for a sculpture-in-motion.

One-half to three-quarter-inch diameter coaxial cable is the large line strung on telephone poles that carries cable TV to a home. When the black plastic covering is removed, a foam-filled silver aluminum coated wire is revealed. This wire is very lightweight and can be bent easily to hold its shape. Think of it as a grown-up version of aluminum clothesline. Cable TV companies are a source for scraps.

Materials of the Trade

Armature	Media		
	PAPIER-MÂCHÉ	PLASTER	FOAM
wire	O	O	O
bamboo	O		O
sculpted paper	O		O
rolled paper	O		
cardboard	O		O
chicken wire	O	O	
balloons	O	O	
wire screen	O	O	
Styrofoam			O
plastic pipe			O
coaxial cable	O		O
urethane foam	O		O
found objects	O	O	
life cast		O	
crumpled foil, paper	O	O	
metal and wood	O		O

Found objects such as hats and cups are especially useful for creating headpieces for urethane foam sculptures. Eyeglasses or cartoon glasses can also be built up with urethane foam. If prop glasses are not available, cut some from cardboard or poster board. Old eyeglass frames can hold a completed mask on your face.

Wire window screen makes an excellent armature for small sculptures of plaster and can be used to add fine details to chicken wire for papier-mâché. Screen can be stretched, creased, folded, unraveled and retied to other pieces. It can be readily shaped by pulling diagonally, which lets it stretch in different directions. Screen wire has enough strength to hold its form and can be combined with other materials for added versatility.

Styrofoam is light and easy to shape into an armature. There are a large number of ready-made geometrics available. Wig heads and solid Styrofoam packing materials are easy to find, as are Styrofoam trays from food packaging.

In addition to its use as a stuffing to build out a sculpture, urethane foam often serves as its own armature. It can be glued together using Japanese origami techniques to hold its own form.

The best way to think of your project is by its armature.

PART TWO

Getting to Work

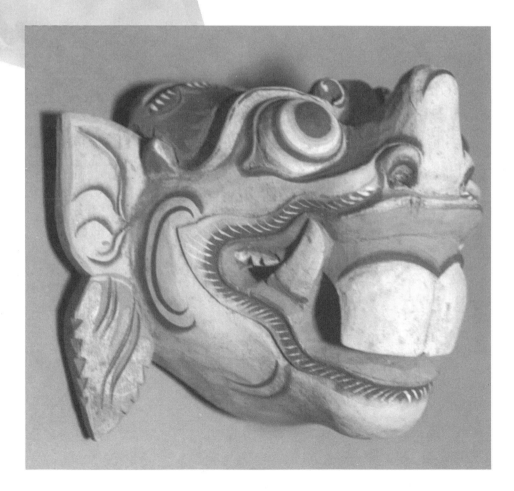

Indonesian Mask used to protect the
wearer from evil spirits. Courtesy
Fred Kahn.

Part Two is a how-to section for creating such sculptures as masks, head-pieces, puppets and creatures—real and imagined. Projects of papier-mâché, plaster and foam are highlighted in each chapter.

The latter chapters are tied to real-life experiences. Exploring these projects can lead to the discovery that there is more to teaching and learning art than the projects themselves. As you and your students work with the lessons, you will find that "teachable moments" are out there; we need to take advantage of them. We need to remember that we, too, are part of the process and that we can learn with and from our students. Real motivation comes from within. We need to set the stage and then not be afraid to let inspiration happen.

the mask

throughout history people have used masks as disguises to hide their personalities, to summon spirits or to give the wearers an aura of magic. The earliest masks were probably animal masks used by hunters to stalk their prey or face-painting intended to scare off enemies.

Later most masks were used in ceremonies, in the theater, in commemorations of the dead or as parts of festivals.

Ceremonial masks derive from the belief that the gods control nature. A masked dancer may take on the identity of a spirit or god in ceremonial rituals. The False Face Society of the Iroquois Indians of North America has traditionally worn fantastic wooden masks to heal the sick and afflicted. The Husk Face Society has made masks of corn husks for the same purpose. Masks have always been important parts of ceremonies of the Kwakiutl Indian secret societies of the Pacific Northwest. Their story-telling masks have moving parts for animation. The Kwakiutl Echo mask has interchangeable mouths to represent different figures during the telling of a tale. The Hopi Indians of Arizona traditionally mask themselves to represent their ancestors, whose spirits are known as *kachinas*. Kachinas are believed to make rain, produce food and even aid in puberty rites.

The ancient Greeks wore masks to enhance their theater. A masked actor might represent a particular god, enabling the god to communicate with the audience. Human emotions such as love, hate, joy and fear could easily be revealed by the actors' masks.

In classic Chinese drama, color-coded masks are used to portray different characters in a play. A type of Japanese play called *No* uses numerous masks, and the Japanese Kabuki Theater uses stylized painted faces to create its masks.

Burial masks were important to the ancient Egyptians for identification. The sarcophagus, or stone coffin, was often fashioned as a mask for the mummy. In Western countries, death masks of historic figures like Napoleon and Beethoven show us what they looked like.

Masks have also been a large part of African art and culture. The Korubla mask from the Ivory Coast has the head of a hyena with the mouth of a crocodile, making it practical for witch chasing.

Carnival mask for Feast of San Juan. Puerto Rico. Papier-mâché. Courtesy Romaldo Gonzalez.

This mask depicting snakes and serpents is used in rain-making ceremonies. Mexico. Wood. Courtesy Romaldo Gonzalez.

The normal head is egg shaped and can be divided roughly into three parts: hairline to eyebrows, brows to nose tip, and nose to chin. The mouth is halfway between the nose and chin. Ears should be aligned with the brows and the tip of the nose. These general human proportions are fine for realistic masks and puppets but should be looked on only as a reference when developing more fanciful characters.

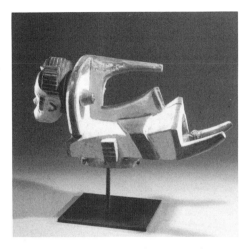

Masks with a raffia fringe have traditionally been made by young men in Zaire as part of initiation into adulthood. The masks show how much they learned during training, sometimes with complicated carvings of everything from leopards to pickup trucks. Some of the masks of the Pende from Zaire are meant to entertain with comedy and satire, generally portraying different character types found in the village.

Festival masks have evolved from religious ceremonies. Harvest festivals have long been popular among American Indian tribes as well as among societies in China, India, Alaska and the South Seas. Carnival and Mardi Gras are celebrated on Shrove Tuesday, the last day before Lent, in countries with Roman Catholic populations, including the United States. Carnival in Rio de Janeiro and Mardi Gras in New Orleans are the most famous of these festivities.

The elaborately costumed Mummers get worldwide attention via television during their annual parades in Philadelphia, at Christmastime in New York and in the football bowl parades in California and Florida. Renaissance and medieval festivals in the United States have become an increasingly popular way to create masquerades for fun or fundraising.

(*Above left*) **This Centipede Kite mask proves that masks are found on kites, too! China. Paper. Courtesy Bill Lockhart and Betty Street, Lubbock, Texas.**

(*Above*) **This anthropomorphic Ibo Elephant mask was called a Wa-Wa mask by African traders. The left side represents Man and the right side represents an elephant. Nigeria, Africa. Courtesy Davis Gallery of African Art, New Orleans, Louisiana.**

(*Left*) **Top: Dan Shirt mask; left and right center: Dan Male masks; bottom: Dan Passport mask. Ivory Coast, Liberia, Africa. Wood, fiber. Courtesy Davis Gallery of African Art, New Orleans, Louisiana.**

The Paper Bag Mask

MATERIALS

brown grocery bag
cardboard, poster board
scissors
wheat paste
newsprint
masking tape
paper towels
kraft paper
tempera paint
paintbrushes

Traditionally masks made from paper bags are among the easiest masks for young children to make and decorate because they require only cutting, pasting and coloring. The addition of papier-mâché

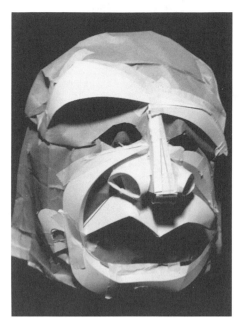

Add scored paper shapes and crumpled paper to build up dramatic forms, like noses, ears and eyebrows.

and create details that can be covered later with papier-mâché. Wadded paper is easily shaped to fill out the armature. Use masking tape to temporarily hold shapes in place until laminated. Apply strips of newsprint soaked in flour or wheat paste to cover all detail areas and any creases or folds. Switch to paper towels for covering larger open areas to speed up the process. Continue alternating layers of newsprint, kraft paper and paper towels. The number of layers should depend on the strength needed or the attention span of the maker. *Remember*, the mask doesn't have to be strong enough for you to stand on it.

When the mask is completely dry, finish it with tempera paint. A final coat of water-soluble polyurethane improves water resistance.

turns the brown grocery bag into one of the most versatile armatures on which to build.

There are two ways to begin making the mask. The open edge of the bag can be rolled up to form a collar for support. As an alternative method, open the bag and cut an arch on each side to fit on your shoulders. The basic shape of the mask can be expanded by pasting or stapling poster board to the bag.

Making your first paper bag mask in an exaggerated or stylized form gives the opportunity to experiment and discover techniques. Scored paper and cardboard can be attached to the bag to build forms

A mask will come alive when you add details and color.

Two ways to use paper bags as masks.

Cut-and-Fold Mask

MATERIALS

poster board

scissors

crayons

wheat paste

newsprint

tape

acrylic modeling paste

joint cement

sandpaper

yarn

fabric

white latex paint

tempera

acrylic or oil-base paint

paintbrushes

This mask uses a simple form as the basis for developing a more elaborate work. When combined with papier-mâché, the basic mask actually becomes the armature for an expanded creation.

Begin with a rectangular piece of paper or poster board about as wide as your head. Fold it in half and cut out a nose triangle. Mark and cut out eyes. Use this mask as the template to design other shapes.

• SAFETY NOTE: To avoid self-inflicted eye injuries, have students work in pairs to mark the eye holes. One student holds the mask to his or her face and points to the eye positions. The second student marks the positions with a crayon or other blunt-tip marker.

If this template is traced on a larger piece of poster board, the excess board can be cut and scored to create the different details and features of a particular character. Let the cut edges describe the creature, knight, warrior or whatever.

Make a paper pattern at the size you want the mask to be and use this to design mask shapes over it.

(Below) Add details to the front of the mask by scoring poster board.

Add details such as noses, lashes and brows by scoring paper or board and taping it in place to create a three-dimensional effect. Now you are ready to expand the mask into a papier-mâché creation.

Apply papier-mâché newsprint strips to the desired thickness and allow the mask to dry (See Chapter One, *The Strip Method*). You are now ready to add texture to the surface. Acrylic modeling paste is excellent to add a rough or built-up texture. For the ambitious artist, joint cement can be applied thinly and sanded to smooth out uneven surfaces. Yarn or fabric can be added to give relief.

The surface treatment of the mask is one of the most important stages of mask building, a design process in its own right. It can make or break the effectiveness of a mask. You might want to add exaggerated textures. Research examples and experiment with line, tone, color, form and texture before you decide on what materials and techniques to use.

Before painting, coat your mask with white latex wall paint as a sealer. Latex is an acrylic, so any tempera, acrylic or oil-base finish can be used for decoration.

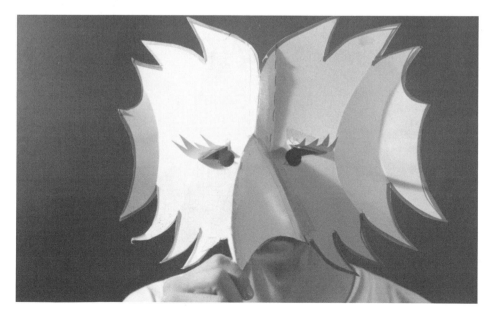

Oodles of doodles helps brainstorm Nose Mask ideas. Try some doodles of your own!

The Nose Mask

MATERIALS

paper
scissors
markers
poster board
newsprint
wheat paste
finishing materials as desired (acrylic or tempera paint, found objects, etc.)

The nose mask is an expanded version of the simple cut-and-fold mask, with a folded-down nose added to enhance the three-dimensional effect.

Compare noses on different animals. Look at children's picture books and encyclopedias, where facial details are often carefully articulated. Sketch noses and compare. Which ones are truly different, and which ones are very much alike? See

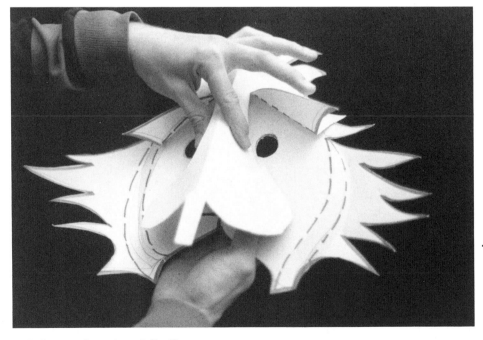

Pull the nose down for a 3-D effect. The length and width of the nose can be adjusted to accommodate the plan.

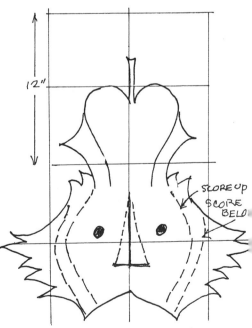

This pattern for a nose mask shows a flap at the top which, when folded down, will become the nose.

if you can discover families of noses so that you can begin with a few bases and vary each slightly to make many. As you sketch each nose, see if you can break it down into its component parts.

Make a small nose mask of paper to use as a template. Try it on and fit the eyes. Now determine what type of creature you want to portray. Will the mask have hair or a beard or mustache? What kind of animal do you want to create?

Once you have decided on your creature, transfer the template shape to poster board. Cut out and assemble the armature. Now add papier-mâché to your armature. When dry, finish with paint, yarn and found objects as desired. It is amazing how many creatures can come from one simple mask.

Modeling a Face in Plasticene

MATERIALS

**Styrofoam wig head or
    crumpled newspaper
plasticene**

The first step in creating a plasticene model is to make an armature. The easiest way is to split a Styrofoam wig head in half to make two basic egg shapes. Wig heads are inexpensive and are frequently found in thrift shops. If a wig head is not available, make an armature out of paper. Crumple sheets of newspaper and tape them tightly together in an egg shape.

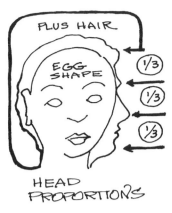

Cover the basic form with a one-quarter-inch layer of plasticene. If the plasticene is too hard, place it in sunlight until softer. Divide the head into proportions of roughly thirds: top of head to brow, brow to tip of nose and nose to chin. Cut a triangular slab of plasticene and build a nose. Add more plasticene to build up the forehead and brows. Develop the mouth area halfway between the nose tip and the chin. Shape it as if a set of teeth were there. Feel your own face and try to simulate the feeling of it in plasticene.

Add details by building up and cutting away until your subject and style of mask has been achieved. Try not to have undercuts so that the model can be removed intact and used over again.

When the plasticene model is complete, the artist may proceed with papier-mâché.

The Lift Mask

MATERIALS

plasticene
mold (Styrofoam wig head, another mask, a
    found object)
aluminum foil
wheat paste
finishing materials as desired (paint, found
    objects, etc.)
Optional: fabric

The lift mask usually begins with a cast from either a plasticene model created especially for the work, a styrofoam wig head, a copy of another mask or a found object. Plasticene has an oily base and acts as its own separator for strip-method papier-mâché. When copying another mask or object, a layer of aluminum foil should be used to ease separation.

It is easier to lift a mask if there are no undercuts (indentations with overhangs) on the model. If your model does have undercuts, the mask can always be cut for removal, then put back together later. The first step is to laminate the model with several layers of papier-mâché. After the papier-mâché dries, remove it from the model. This is your basic lift. Use paste-soaked crushed paper towels to build up form. Sculpted, or scored, paper details can be taped in position, then covered with mâché strips. Paint, texture and other surface treatments should do the rest.

Building up form and details in this way on a store-bought plastic mask can turn it into a dramatic creation of your own. Or you can scavenger for other objects that simulate a base mask shape and add parts of plasticene or other materials. A papier-mâché cast is then made from this assemblage. In any case, don't forget to decide whether the style of the mask will be realistic, imaginary, exaggerated or stylized. The way you finish the mask can determine the style and whole appearance of the final product.

The armatures for these half masks are made from sculpted paper and plasticene. The nose is the most important part.

The Half Mask

MATERIALS

Styrofoam wig head
stuffed paper egg shape or sculpted paper
    armature
aluminum foil
paper
pencil
wheat paste
newsprint
masking tape
plasticene
poster board
finishing materials as desired (acrylic or
    tempera paint, found objects, etc.)

Once again the easiest armature is the split Styrofoam wig head or stuffed paper egg, except that this time only the top half will be used—à la half mask.

Cover at least the top half of the mold with aluminum foil for easy separation, then decide what beast or creature you want the mask to portray. It could be a chicken, crow or cockatoo, a dog, cat or even a pig.

The dominant feature on the half mask is the nose. Many theater makeup artists actually use only a painted nose and a few detailed lines to turn an actor into an animal. The same emphasis is called for in creating half masks, but the mask edges can also enhance the development of the creatures.

Shapes. Sketch a variety of noses (See *The Nose Mask*, p. 46). Draw a general head shape around each and locate ears. For example, a cat's head might be diamond shape, while a pig's would be round.

The armature might differ from animal to animal. The hooked nose of a bird could be attached to a Styrofoam wig head and a positive cast made of papier-mâché. Sculpted paper would work well for the base of a pig's or cat's head with the appropriate nose attached. After the papier-mâché is dry, cut underneath and reclaim the plasticene. Finish the mask as desired.

Fabric mâché. Substitute fabric for paper in the mâché while adding more white glue to the paste. An effective technique is to use paper strips for the first coats and switch to fabric for the last. Fabric layers improve a mask's durability, particularly if it will be handled a lot.

Balloon Mask

MATERIALS

balloons
wheat paste
kraft paper
newsprint
paper towels
poster board
scissors
cardboard
paper cups
finishing materials as desired (paint, found objects, etc.)

The most important step in creating a balloon mask is to inflate a balloon and tie a secure knot that does not leak. If you want an elongated pear shape, fill the balloon with water and hang it up by its knotted end while working on it.

Dip paper towel strips into *water only* and cover the surface of the whole balloon. This will prevent the papier-mâché from sticking to the balloon surface when the balloon later deflates.

Layer strips of papier-mâché on the balloon letting strips overlap from different directions. Alternate layers of newsprint and kraft paper to gain strength and control of coverage.

When dry, you have a choice: make either one whole-head mask or divide the sphere into two face masks. Converting to two face masks allows younger children to work as teams during the tedious process of layering papier-mâché.

Build mask features with cardboard, paper scoring, layered crumpled paper or paper cups and cover with more strips and paste. Allow to dry and finish as desired.

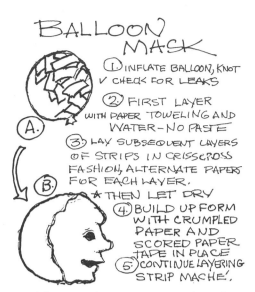

BALLOON MASK

1. INFLATE BALLOON, KNOT & CHECK FOR LEAKS
2. FIRST LAYER WITH PAPER TOWELING AND WATER – NO PASTE
3. LAY SUBSEQUENT LAYERS OF STRIPS IN CRISSCROSS FASHION, ALTERNATE PAPERS FOR EACH LAYER. THEN LET DRY
4. BUILD UP FORM WITH CRUMPLED PAPER AND SCORED PAPER TAPE IN PLACE
5. CONTINUE LAYERING STRIP MACHE.

CUT IN HALF FOR TWO OR MAKE WHOLE HEAD

Balloon mask.

Surgical Gauze Face Masks

MATERIALS

shower cap or headband
large cloth or sheets of paper
solid vegetable shortening
petroleum jelly
plaster surgical gauze
plaster
acrylic or oil-base paint
varnish

The most obvious armature to use for making a mask is the human face because it is readily available and assures the maker of a good fit. The surgical gauze mask, in which the human face is actually the mold and the mask becomes the cast, can be made by middle and high school students.

Preparation. Cover as much of the model's hair as possible with a shower cap or wide headband. Cover the model's upper body with a large cloth or paper jumpsuit. Lubricate brows, lashes and other facial hair with petroleum jelly or solid vegetable shortening. The shortening washes off easier than petroleum jelly, but either works well. Moisturizing skin lotion can be spread on skin surfaces to keep them moist and protect them.

Always communicate with your model and let him or her know what you are doing. Try to describe what the model's eyes can't see. Give the model a pencil and pad for communication. The artist must make certain that the model feels comfortable throughout the process.

Make a Cast. Cut plaster gauze in two-inch strips, six or eight inches long, mak-

ing certain to cut all the strips you'll need before applying any to the model. One at a time, dip the strips in water and apply them to the face, allowing strips to overlap in different directions for strength. Continue layering strips until you have attained enough thickness for the basic mask form. Roll some strips triple thick lengthwise and frame your mask around the edges. Plaster gauze becomes slightly warm as it hardens, which helps signal when the cast is ready to remove.

•**SAFETY NOTE:** Leave the model's nostrils clear for breathing and remind the model not to open his or her eyes. Eye pads applied before covering with gauze may help make the model more comfortable. Young children's eyes should not be covered for casting; their masks should be made eyeless.

Make the mask only a few layers thick and add additional layers later. This leaves the mask flexible and easier to remove. Lift the mask off slowly by working your fingers around the edges first and asking the model to wiggle facial features. Help the model rinse residue from eyelashes and face, making certain that eyes aren't irritated by rubbing.

For fun. Look at the inside of the mask as you shine a light up from the bottom. The face will appear in 3-D, because you will see a positive image of a negative shape.

The gauze mask can be an end in itself, as it was for George Segal (See Chapter Two, p. 12), or you can build and expand on it. The gauze mask could become the armature for a completely different mask—maybe even a wild thing.

Finish with a protective coat of acrylic or varnish to supply added strength and water resistance.

Cover the model's hair with a shower cap and lubricate other facial hair with petroleum jelly or vegetable shortening.

Laminate layers of plaster gauze strips.
Don't forget to leave the mask nostrils open
for breathing!

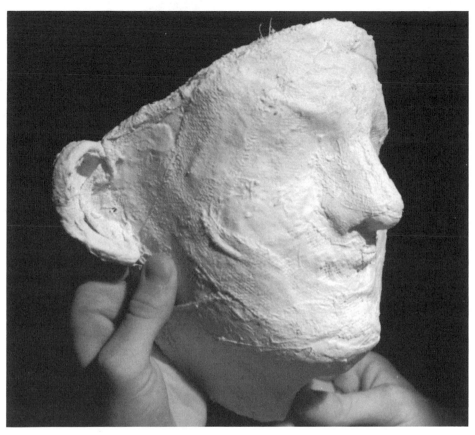

Now you have a mask that is a replica of
the model's face.

Carefully work the mask loose from the
model's eyes and brows. Walk the model to
a sink and rinse any residue from his or her
eyes and face.

Masks as Wall Hangings

MATERIALS

several surgical gauze masks

half-inch plywood

plaster surgical gauze or plaster and
  textured fabric

tempera

acrylics or varnish

Creating a wall hanging of masks entails trying to find a new form for a virtual collage of pieces and parts.

Arrange a group of surgical gauze masks on a flat base of half-inch plywood. Cut parts of some masks and rearrange together to form new shapes. Fill in empty spaces with surgical plaster gauze or textured fabric dipped in plaster. Finish with tempera or acrylic paint or varnish.

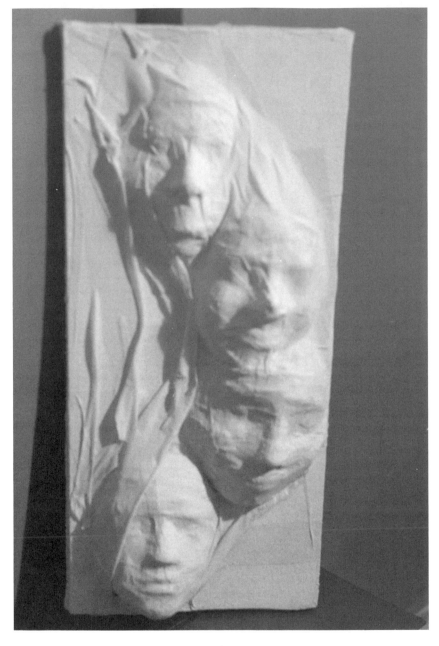

Wall hanging: plaster gauze masks draped with fabric.

Sand Casting

MATERIALS

a box

sand

water

various household tools (rasps, spoons, scoops, nails, gears, screwdrivers, washers, etc.)

plaster

hanger

Sand castings can be used as masks, wall hangings, relief sculptures, murals and interior and exterior wall treatments.

Sand molds, like sand castles at the beach, have short lives. They can only be used once before being reclaimed to begin the cycle again. Sand castings are easy to make and only require a little sand, plaster, water and a few household tools.

Begin with a box to hold the sand. It can be wood, cardboard or a frame with a plastic liner. Pour a thick layer of sand into the box, and wet the sand just enough to hold up the edges of your impressions. Make a test impression to see if the edges hold up. Lay out your design and begin to press it into the sand using various household tools and objects such as spoons, screwdrivers, nails, gears and rasps. Remember that a raised area in the mold will be depressed in the cast and any excavation will appear in relief. Also keep in mind that the frailty of a sand mold will not accommodate delicate designs.

When the mold is finished, mix plaster to the consistency of heavy cream. Generally you should pour in the plaster from one end of the mold. If there are deep areas, spoon in plaster there first, then pour from the end. If there are narrow or thin areas in the cast, place a piece of wire screen or a rod in the indentation for strength. Place a hanger or two for mounting. Simply imbed one or two wire loops in back while the plaster is still wet.

Allow the piece to dry overnight. Carefully dig out the cast and brush off all loose sand. You can still scrape away any areas that you want to contrast with the natural sand quality.

Shapes pressed into a box of damp sand will be raised on the plaster casting.

Brush off excess sand to reveal the finished mask.

Clay Casting

MATERIALS

paper
pencil
plasticene clay
various household tools
plaster
cardboard
plastic sheet
hanger

Clay casting is a process similar to sand casting, substituting clay for sand as the mold medium.

Sketch a general face shape with paper and pencil, and determine the contours of the edges. Experiment with pressing all sorts of household tools into clay. It is important to use plasticene clay because its oil base acts as a separator. In a slab of plasticene, dig out the shapes that you want raised in relief. If you want the eye holes to be empty, stick two banana-shaped cylinders into the clay so they extend above the level of the plaster to be poured. Use the tools to apply textures to the plasticene in character with the mask. Clay molds are not as frail as sand molds, so your details and textures can be more delicate. Build a cardboard wall around the slab and seal any leaks. Begin with a milk coat, or thin coat, of plaster. Then build up a concave surface. Add hangers.

The Draped Mask

MATERIALS

Dip 'N' Drape or cotton muslin or other thin fabric
Styrofoam head or other armature
assorted found objects
fabric
plaster

"Soaked to the skin" sums up the appearance of the draped mask and describes how it is made. Begin with an armature. You could use a store-bought plastic mask stuffed with wadded newspaper to hold the shape or a Styrofoam head if a more realistic style is desired. An imaginary or exaggerated mask could be created by beginning with a base and building up a relief with all sorts of found objects (paper cups, beads, ribbons, etc.) to develop the form. Use a separator where needed. Cut the fabric into strips. If using Dip 'N' Drape, follow product preparation directions. If using other fabric, dip the strips into plaster. Apply the strips over the armature, smoothing the contours as you go. After laminating a couple of layers, allow the mask to dry thoroughly. Varnish and paint as desired.

(Below) **A lift is created from a store-bought mask covered with Dip 'N' Drape, then embellished.**

Wonderwall, designed by Post-Modern architect Charles Moore as a centerpiece for the 1984 World's Fair in New Orleans, successfully turned unsightly high tension wires into a fantasy world. The wall was sculpted in Styrofoam, then covered with fiberglass mesh and topped with Dryvit Primus Adhesive and Top Coat for permanence.

(Above) Charles Moore (for Perez, Ernst, Farnet), *Wonderwall*. Styrofoam, Dryvit, approximately 2300' (701 m) x up to 3 stories. Collection of August Perez. Photograph by Alan Karchner.

(Left) *Wonderwall* at night, detail.

Ida Kohlmeyer, *Arboreal*. Although this piece is made of wood, it is an example of what can be made as an outdoor sculpture using Styrofoam with the Dryvit system. Wood, 15 1/4" x 9 3/4" x 2 3/4" (38.8 x 24.8 x 7 cm). Collection of the artist.

Barth Brothers, a New Orleans design studio operated by Joe and Barry Barth, exemplifies sculpture as a business profession. The studio designs and builds Mardi Gras floats and large decorative sculpture for shopping malls and commercial establishments. Its works include *Riverwalk*, New Orleans; *Arizona Center*, Phoenix; *Underground Atlanta*; and the *Rouse Centers* in Baltimore and Miami.

(**Above**) Barth Brothers, Mardi Gras float. The basic structure of a float can be recycled year after year. New sculptures and background are made to follow changing themes.
Approximately 40' x 10' x 17' 6" (12 x 3 x 5.3 m). Photograph by Barry Barth.

(**Left**) When this giant head is lowered into position, it will be secured much like a prow ornament on an old sailing vessel. Papier-mâché. Photograph by Barry Barth.

(Above, right) Joe Barth III, *Baroque Catfish*. Papier-mâché, 10' x 15' x 15' (3 x 4.6 x 4.6 m).

(Above) Barth Brothers, *Head of Medusa*. Papier-mâché, 12' x 12' x 12' (3.7 x 3.7 x 3.7 m).

(Right) View inside Barth Brothers studio showing props in progress.

Red Grooms and his Ruckus Construction Crew idealized art as collaboration in 1967, when Grooms invented the sculpto-picto-rama. The construction of these mixed-media, three-dimensional environments peaked in 1976 with *Ruckus Manhattan*. From preliminary sketches through lightening construction, the Ruckus crew scurried in helter-skelter fashion, gobbling up art supplies and building materials along the way. Each of Grooms' installations are built to withstand the thousands of mesmerized viewers who walk through and around his lurching buildings and kooky characters.

Red Grooms, Ruckus Manhattan: Woolworth Building. This parody of Frank W. Woolworth's "Five and Dime" philosophy features a life-size revolving door, through which viewers may pass into a mosaic-laden lobby. Mixed media, 17' x 14' x 15' (5.2 x 4.3 x 4.6 m). Courtesy Red Grooms/Marlborough.

Woolworth Building (detail). Mr. Woolworth himself shows a chunk of his Gothic tower to passers-by.

Red Grooms, *Ruckus Rodeo*. In the midst of *Manhattan* mayhem, Grooms and his crew created this commission for the Modern Art Museum of Fort Worth: an interpretation of Fort Worth's annual Fat Stock Show and Rodeo. Mixed media, 16' x 100' x 30' (4.9 x 30.5 x 9 m). Courtesy Modern Art Museum of Fort Worth, purchased and commissioned with funds from the National Endowment for the Arts and The Benjamin J. Tillar Memorial Trust.

Highlights of student work in papier-mâché and urethane foam, courtesy Isidore Newman School (New Orleans) and author/art teacher George Wolfe.

(Left) It all started with a paper bag. A wide variety of masks can be made from grocery bags, papier-mâché and bright colors.

(Below) This 20' (6 m) mini-float called *The Bad Seed* was built by high school students for the Krewe of Clones parade. The papier-mâché beast, with his oozing volcano and pink cloud, was funded by a grant from the National Endowment for the Arts through the Contemporary Art Center, New Orleans.

Anyone wearing this many-headed hydra will be the center of attention. Urethane foam on a back pack frame, 6' x 12' x 12' (1.8 x 3.7 x 3.7 m).

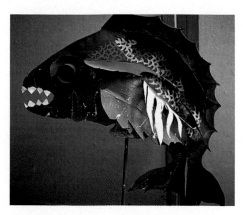

(Above) Ruckus Middle Kingdom? Red Grooms may have some competition for the spotlight. Teacher-student collaboration in papier-mâché and urethane foam. Photograph by Rose Doumitt.

(Left) An awesome fish headpiece. Papier-mâché. Student work by Joey Darlak.

Since its fifteenth-century beginning, life-casting in plaster has found flexibility in composition and its means of expression. The use of plaster gauze and, more recently, alginate have expanded the potential of plaster as a life-casting medium in the fine arts.

(**Above**) George Segal, *The Dancers*. Segal uses plaster gauze to cast his actors, then arranges them to make a statement. 5' 10 1/2" x 8' 10" x 5' 11" (1.79 x 2.69 x 1.8 m). Courtesy National Gallery of Art, Gift of the Collectors Committee.

(**Right**) Willa Shalit and Dean Ericson, *Rower's Torso*. The artists used alginate to mold a life-like impression, then made a plaster cast. They often mold and cast selected fragments to create their personal view. This piece has been re-cast in bronze. Life-size. Courtesy College of Santa Fe.

Direct Sculpted Mask

MATERIALS

Elmer's SAF-T Contact Cement or 3M #30
    NF Contact Cement
large paintbrush
large sheets of kraft paper
plastic mask or Styrofoam head
newsprint
wheat paste
white glue
water
acrylic paint
tempera
polymer medium

This approach, which is a variation of the lift mask (see page 48), is relatively new

and only possible using special water-soluble contact cements.

Using a big paintbrush, apply a thin coat of Elmer's SAF-T Contact Cement or 3M #30 NF Contact Cement on large sheets of brown kraft paper. A plastic mask or a Styrofoam head acts as a quick armature. Tear the kraft paper into pieces and apply them to the surface of the armature. Each new piece should overlap and stick to the previous one until a form is made. Crumple up the leftover adhesive-coated paper and add to the form as desired. Let the mask cure and harden substantially overnight. Remove the mask from the armature. You can also wad more kraft paper and stick it to the mask to build up the form even more. Refine shapes into more finished forms. Let the mask cure overnight again. Laminate strips of traditional papier-mâché (newsprint strips, wheat paste, water, white glue) to give a solid, hard, water-resistant body.

Once the mask has dried it's ready to finish. Think about the effect or mood you want the mask to reflect, and select your color scheme using acrylic or tempera colors mixed with polymer medium.

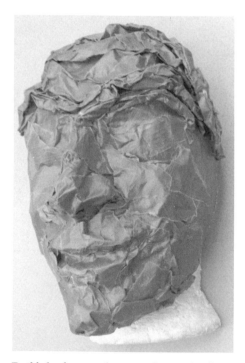

Build the form up by crumpling and rolling paper coated with contact cement until the form is revealed.

Artist Russell Elliot used contact mâché and cardboard to make this horned warrior.

Foam Creature Masks

MATERIALS

paper or cardboard
pencil
scissors
urethane foam
Aleene's Thick Designer Tacky Glue
pushpins

Urethane foam is an excellent medium for creating quick face masks. While it is not as durable as papier-mâché, urethane foam can be more easily manipulated to create variations from a few basic shapes. By adding or subtracting parts, you can make many masks out of one basic shape.

A circle shape can be used for any round-faced animal, depending on the length of nose. Using pencil, paper or cardboard and scissors, make a template to experiment with multiple animals.

Begin with a circle approximately sixteen inches in diameter and locate the eyes. Make cuts in the top and bottom as shown. Cut a nose triangle, fold it and glue it to the circle with Aleene's Thick Designer Tacky Glue. See Chapter Three for other adhesive options. Pin the mask to the wall while the glue dries.

To create a bird mask, cut a nose like a beak and describe the feathers with the mask's outside edges. Cut and glue eyebrows, lashes and hair to the mask. For a dog mask, fold a triangle nose under and tie a knot around the end. Add appropriate ears, depending on the type of dog, and

maybe a tongue. To make a bulldog, glue valley folds in the nose triangle, creating wrinkles and a shorter nose.

A bear can be fashioned by shortening and widening the nose triangle slightly. Tie the nose and valley fold on dotted lines to shape the mask. Cut the outside edge to describe the bear's fur. Cut small triangles for ears, and add a tongue and other details as desired. Try dropping the bottom jaw for an awesome effect. Add a mane and create a lion.

The round mask can be varied or extended to create an endless parade of imaginative wild things. The process remains the same: cut a basic shape. Add a nose, hair, fur or feathers. Cut out teeth and brows, and add other desired details.

Cut a one-and-a-half-inch strip, double it over and glue it to make piping. Piping is great for outlining and detailing.

Creature masks can be as wild as your imagination.

(Opposite) **The universal parts of the foam mask allow you to build an entire menagerie of animals. One mask can have many interchangeable parts.**

CREATURE MASKS

PATTERN FOR MANY MASKS

TEETH
CUT TWO AT ONE TIME

←16"→

BROW

SCORE ON BOTTOM
TONGUE

HAIR

NOSE

NOSTRIL

MANE

PIPING

FOR DETAILING
FOLD OVER A STRIP AND GLUE

EARS

PUT GLUE ON DOTTED LINES AND FOLD IN TO GIVE SHAPE TO THE FACE

FRONT   SIDE

BIRD

GLUE ON SAME NOSE SHAPE, BUT BEND DOWN TIP AND TIE STRING TO MAKE NOSE
+ ADD TONGUE

KNOT

FRONT   DOG   SIDE

BULLDOG

MAKE THE NOSE SHAPE A LITTLE LONGER

FOLD UNDER AND GLUE FOR WRINKLES

BEND DOWN TIP AND TIE WITH STRING FOR NOSE

VARIATIONS OF A CREATURE MASK

VARY THE CUT OF EDGE

MAKE THE NOSE A LITTLE WIDER

BEAR

ADD A MANE TO A DOG AND YOU HAVE A LION

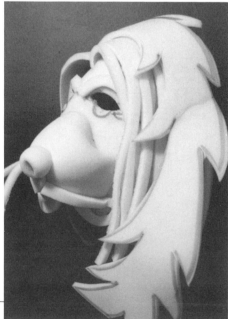

Sandwich Mask

urethane foam

scissors

Aleene's Thick Designer Tacky Glue

clothespins

pushpins

finishing materials as desired (spray paint, buttons, yarn, etc.)

The sandwich mask derives its name from the way it's made: by gluing together two large pieces of foam that will fit over a person's head. The head and upper part of the wearer's body is the armature, or filling of the sandwich.

Glue the edges of each piece of foam together, leaving an opening for the head at the bottom, and hold in place with clothespins until the glue has dried. Slide the mask over the wearer's head and locate the eyes. Remember that the basic mask will be a great deal larger than the wearer's head and the eye holes will probably fall far below the mask's eye. Cut and add details of foam, but don't cover the eyeholes! Tack the mask to a wall until dry. Finish with spray paint, buttons, yarn or other materials, and allow for ample drying time as needed.

Head Mask

MATERIALS

urethane foam

Aleene's Thick Designer Tacky Glue

finishing materials as desired (yarn, pipe cleaners, buttons, etc.)

Cut a rectangular shape a little over three times the width of your head to make a cylinder that fits. Glue the edges together and allow the cylinder to dry. Add a top and locate eyes. Finish the mask with paint or interesting glued-on materials (See Chapter Three).

the headpiece

Note the sculptural quality of these headpieces from Cameroon. Left: Bomileke Civil Cat. Right: Bomileke Leopard. Courtesy of Davis Gallery of African Art, New Orleans, Louisiana.

What is a headpiece? Is it really different than a mask? Many artists use these terms interchangeably because throughout history the purposes for creating them have been the same. This makes sense as long as you only read or study about them, but as you begin to build both you will find a natural division delineated by the way the armatures are made.

For the purposes of this book, the mask is defined as a facial covering or relief sculpture and the headpiece as a combination of mask, hat or helmet with the three-dimensional quality of sculpture-in-the-round. Some headpieces are conceived as masks of the head while others, such as traditional Chinese dragons or the huge walking heads of France, encompass the whole body.

As with all projects, making a headpiece requires thoughtful planning. Begin by forming a design concept. Do some brainstorming with the class, and research the ways headpieces have been used in different cultures throughout history. Sketch some ideas for your own headpiece. Review the options for an armature and choose the best media for the job.

The schoolyard is the place where the wild
things are. Isidore Newman School, New
Orleans, Louisiana.

Sculpted Paper

MATERIALS

paper
pencil
poster board
newsprint
wheat paste
white glue
water
tape
Styrofoam wig or crumpled paper egg head
straight pins
finishing materials as desired (paint, yarn,
    feathers, other found materials)

Think of your work as sculpture-in-the-round. The cutting, folding and scoring techniques of sculpted paper produce clean geometric armature shapes with an emphasis on structure.

Begin by sketching animal heads as a series of cartoon-like circles, rectangles and cones. This exercise will give you a feeling for the technique. See how many animals you can simplify like this.

Use a Styrofoam wig or crumpled paper egg head as a structure to build your armatures. When you sketch the animal you plan to build as a headpiece, design it two inches larger than your model to allow for making it three-dimensional and slipping it easily off the Styrofoam head. Fit the headpiece more closely later.

Cut details such as noses and ears from poster board and tape them in place. When the basic armature is complete, remove it from the head structure and try it on. Make adjustments to fit.

Apply papier-mâché strips to the armature, concentrating on the seams and scored areas. These are the tension points

and they need to be strong. Allow the headpiece to dry and finish it with paint and glued-on materials as desired.

Unicorn. This popular motif in mythology is easy to make. Cut a nose from poster board and pin it on a Styrofoam head, cutting slots for nostrils and bending over the front of the nose in the shape of a horse's muzzle. Cut out a neck, mane and pair of cheeks. Tape the parts together. Add details such as eyes, ears and horn. Then papier-mâché.

Rabbit. The armature for a rabbit headpiece can be made the same way you made a nose mask (p. 46) with the addition of a headband to support it.

Sketch a rabbit face shape on poster board using the space between the ears for a nose. Bend the nose down and tape it in position, then cut and tuck the nostrils. Make scores and cuts in the sides of the face, then fold and tack for a three-dimensional effect. Score lines on the backs of the ears and fold.

Use two two-inch strips to make a headband and attach it to the mask. The armature is ready for papier-mâché. If the nose layout seems too difficult, cut the nose shape, score, fold and tape it on.

Bird. Create an eagle, cardinal or other bird with a large beak. Keep your own head in mind as you vary the proportions of head and beak as necessary. Give eyes extra depth by scoring and bending before attaching. When you have completed the armature, apply papier-mâché.

Mouse. This headpiece is made like a helmet. Instead of being just a head, it becomes a stylized mouse with tail.

This approach is effective if the headpiece is used without a formal costume. As part of a costume it might conflict or duplicate parts. For example, the rabbit headpiece could be constructed as a whole bunny with the addition of a cotton tail, but if the headpiece were worn as part of a bunny costume, such treatment would be redundant. Consider the purpose of your piece when choosing an approach.

Lay a sketch of a mouse head shape on a 10" x 14" piece of poster board and draw around it. Attach a headband of poster board strips to the rear, one horizontal to connect the sides and one from the horizontal headband to the top of the mask. To close up the head, add a notched three-inch strip below, like a skirt.

Cut out and score a tail. Cut flaps and use them to attach the tail to the rear of the mask. Last cut and fold the ears and attach them. For extra depth, cut and score the eyes. Apply papier-mâché when your armature is finished.

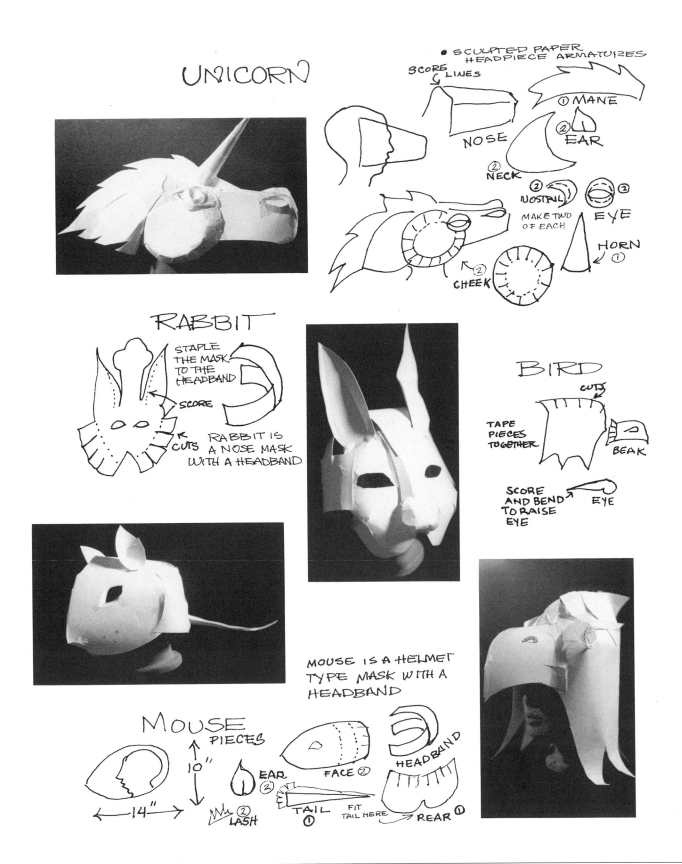

UNICORN

• SCULPTED PAPER
HEADPIECE ARMATURES

SCORE LINES

NOSE

① MANE

② EAR

② NECK

② NOSTRIL

② EYE

① HORN

② CHEEK

MAKE TWO OF EACH

RABBIT

STAPLE THE MASK TO THE HEADBAND

SCORE

CUTS

RABBIT IS A NOSE MASK WITH A HEADBAND

BIRD

CUTS

TAPE PIECES TOGETHER

BEAK

SCORE AND BEND TO RAISE EYE

EYE

MOUSE IS A HELMET TYPE MASK WITH A HEADBAND

MOUSE PIECES

10"

14"

EAR ②

② LASH

FACE ②

TAIL ①

FIT TAIL HERE

HEADBAND

REAR ①

The Great Paper Hat Headpiece

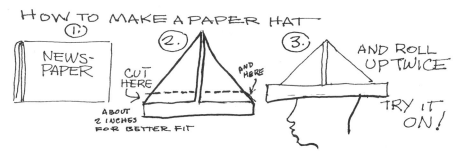

HOW TO MAKE A PAPER HAT

1. NEWS-PAPER

2. CUT HERE · AND HERE · ABOUT 2 INCHES FOR BETTER FIT

3. AND ROLL UP TWICE · TRY IT ON!

MATERIALS

newspapers

scissors

pencil

paper

poster board

stapler

tape

wheat paste

water

latex

tempera

colored and clear spray enamel

glue

found objects as desired (paper plates, foam cups, feathers, etc.)

The classic folded-newspaper hat made by generations of children serves as a simple armature that can spawn countless variations. This method of sculpture is a combination of origami and papier-mâché.

Begin by folding over four sheets of newspaper. Find the center and fold into two equal triangles. Make a two-inch cut on the crease, starting at the opening and aiming toward the peak of the hat. Roll up the two-inch bottom flaps on each side.

The hat can be worn with the top ridge either running front to back or side to side. The creature headpiece you choose to make with this armature will dictate the orientation. Birds, horses and alligators would usually be made from front to back, while crabs and one-eyed Cyclopes probably need to be sideways.

Using paper and pencil, design a pattern for your creature. Lay it out on poster board. Cut out the various parts, and staple and tape them to the paper hat. If you have chosen the crab or the crawfish as your creature, you will see that the claw construction technique is the same for both. The weight of the claws on the crab headpiece adds a twist which makes them more realistic. Those attached to the crawfish are more stable because they are mounted below the hat.

When the basic armature is complete, mix wheat paste and water to a paste consistency. Dip newspaper strips into the paste and cover all seams and joints. Use crisscross strips for added strength. Hang or support the sculpture to dry. Try it on.

Paint the entire sculpture with latex as a sealer. Hang or support it again to dry. Paint with tempera, letting your imagination go wild, adding details and accents. Rehang or support the headpiece to dry. If desired, add shading with spray enamel.

Add any embellishment at hand to dress up your creation. Small paper plates and paper or foam cups can be glued on to make distinctive eyes. Cover the finished sculpture completely with clear enamel spray for added strength and water resistance. Now you are ready for the big show.

The Dragonbird headpiece illustrated here and on pages 67–68 utilizes many of the techniques common to most creatures created with a paper hat armature.

THE CRAB

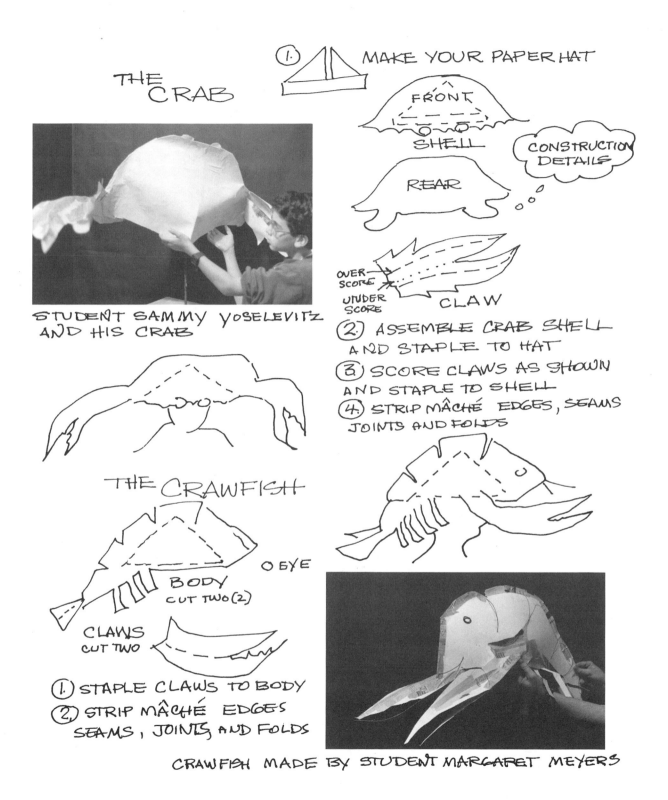

① MAKE YOUR PAPER HAT

FRONT
SHELL
REAR

CONSTRUCTION DETAILS

OVER SCORE
UNDER SCORE
CLAW

STUDENT SAMMY YOSELEVITZ AND HIS CRAB

② ASSEMBLE CRAB SHELL AND STAPLE TO HAT

③ SCORE CLAWS AS SHOWN AND STAPLE TO SHELL

④ STRIP MÂCHÉ EDGES, SEAMS JOINTS AND FOLDS

THE CRAWFISH

O EYE

BODY
CUT TWO (2)

CLAWS
CUT TWO

① STAPLE CLAWS TO BODY
② STRIP MÂCHÉ EDGES SEAMS, JOINTS AND FOLDS

CRAWFISH MADE BY STUDENT MARGARET MEYERS

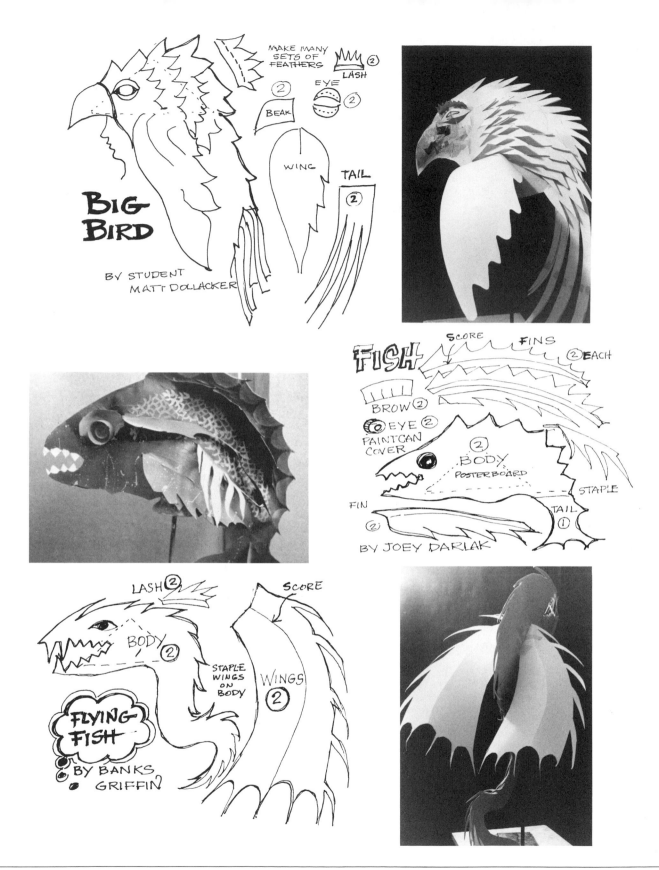

Getting to Work

1. Start by making a simple paper hat from a few sheets of newspaper. Cut and adjust it to fit the wearer.

2. Design the pattern for the bird. Lay it out on poster board.

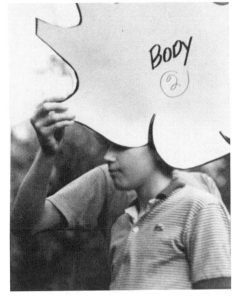

3. Cut and staple the wings. Cut the body large enough to hide the paper hat. Staple the wings to it. Then tape the whole piece to the hat.

4. Cut and fold the beak in origami style and staple it to the hat body. Cut and staple the eyebrows, then tape them to the body.

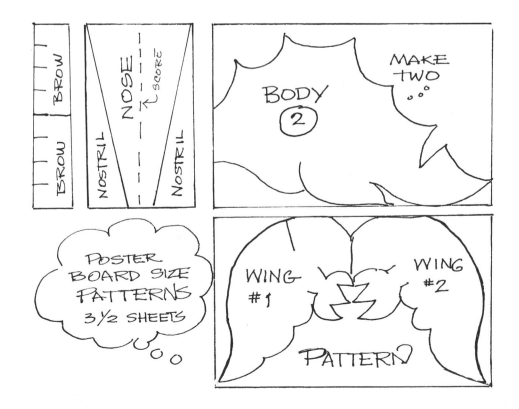

5. Use strips of newspaper dipped in mâché paste to cover all the seams and joints of the bird. Use crisscross strips to secure the wings. When the papier-mâché is complete, hang or support the headpiece until dry. Try it on.

6. Paint the entire bird with latex. Hang or support until dry, making sure the wings hang the way you want them to appear when finished.

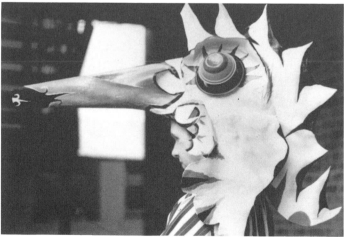

7. Paint the bird with tempera. Rehang the headpiece. When dry, add some shading with spray enamel, then completely cover the bird with a clear enamel spray.

8. Small paper plates and paper or foam cups can be glued on to make very distinctive eyes. Add any embellishments at hand to dress up your creation.

Walking Heads

MATERIALS

corrugated cardboard

scissors

corrugated paper

kraft paper

3M #30 NF Contact Cement

Elmer's SAF-T Contact Cement

wooden sticks

white glue

water

newsprint

finishing materials as desired (paint, found objects, etc.)

A walking head consists of two parts, the base and the head. The design of the base is critical because it determines how the head fits on the carrier.

The overall concept is similar to that of football shoulder pads with a long neck. Weight, support and leverage must be considered. The head must be light but strong, and wind resistance is also an important factor.

The base (neck) should be shaped with arches for the shoulders and extensions down the chest and back for support. Design the base so the sculpture's center of gravity will line up with the center of the wearer's body and head.

Prepare your materials ahead of time so they will be ready to use when needed.

The base is built up with layers of brown paper and corrugated paper or cardboard laminated together with contact cement. Brush on a coat of 3M #30 NF Contact Cement, or Elmer's SAF-T Contact Cement (nontoxic), and let dry. Kraft paper dries in about one-half hour, but corrugated paper and cardboard are more absorbent and need longer drying time.

• SAFETY NOTE: Wear safety goggles and work outside or in a well-ventilated space whenever you work with 3M #30 NF Contact Cement. It contains a solvent and may otherwise irritate eyes and skin.

To build the head, begin by cutting a template from corrugated cardboard in the shape of a silhouette of the head selected. Attach two wooden sticks to the template to hold it upright. Apply contact cement to the perimeter of the template for easy construction.

Cut the dried corrugated cardboard into two-inch and longer strips and begin to build your shape. Round out your template by building a hollow shell of overlapping strips. Continue building until the general form is attained. Then switch to corrugated paper cut into one-inch strips and begin to fill in and tie together the details. After the details are established, begin to layer pieces of kraft paper to smooth out the surface. The last layers should be newsprint strips with white glue and water as the paste. These layers smooth out the surface while ending with a permanent, water-resistant finish. Paint and decorate the head as desired.

Artist Julian Strock with the walking head of *Davey, the Sailor Man.*

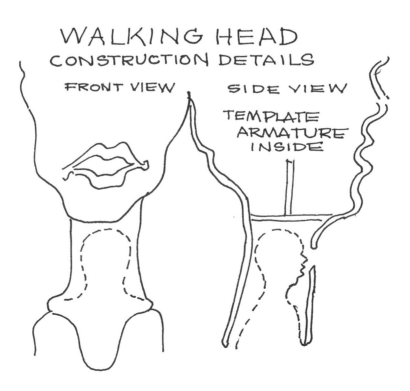

WALKING HEAD
CONSTRUCTION DETAILS
FRONT VIEW   SIDE VIEW
TEMPLATE
ARMATURE
INSIDE

The Baseball Cap Armature

MATERIALS

baseball cap

cardboard

scissors

urethane foam

Aleene's Thick Designer Tacky Glue

found objects as desired (paper cups and
plates, etc.)

paint

clothespins

Here is a great way to start a sculpture—
with an artifact of that great American
pastime, baseball. The baseball cap makes
an accessible, inexpensive base for creating urethane foam creatures.

Cut and glue a piece of cardboard to
extend the bill of the cap. Cut two identical side pieces of foam to resemble the
creature you want to make, such as a dragon. Cut a nose, snout or beak of foam
wider than the cardboard piece extending
the bill, and glue it on. Glue down the
edges first, letting it puff up in the middle.
Add teeth, eyes and other features cut
from foam or fashioned with found objects
such as paper plates and cups. Paint brows
and nostrils, and use piping to outline lips
and other features. Clip the glued parts
together with clothespins until dry.

This method works well for creating
such animals as a horse, unicorn or alligator. Shorten the beak and you can have a
dog, cat, eagle or even a sparrow. Take any
general shape and add different parts.

Any old hat can become an armature.
The construction helmet, for example,
can be the basis for a much larger foam
headpiece. Dad's old fishing hat can support an expanded brim of cardboard.

Conceptual Exercise

If you have never done *origami*, or Japanese paper folding, it would be helpful to
warm up with a conceptual exercise. To
make a swan, begin with a three-inch
square piece of paper and fold as if making a paper airplane. Follow the progres-
sion shown in the illustration from left to
right. Grasp the point and fold it back to
create the neck of the swan. Now grasp
the tail and mountain-valley (accordion)
fold to form a duck's or swan's tail.

Use old baseball caps to make a wide
variety of headpieces. Styrofoam cups, or
whatever found objects seem suitable, make
dramatic eyes.

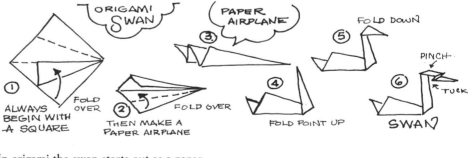

In origami the swan starts out as a paper
airplane. Once you understand this
Japanese paper folding technique urethane
foam will work the same way.

ANY OLD HAT

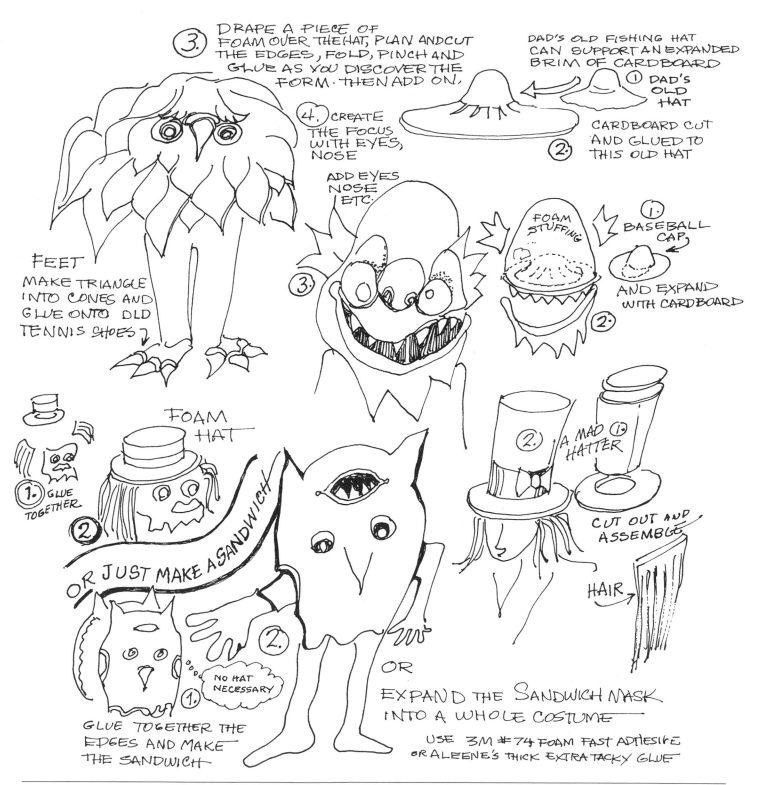

③ DRAPE A PIECE OF FOAM OVER THE HAT, PLAN AND CUT THE EDGES, FOLD, PINCH AND GLUE AS YOU DISCOVER THE FORM. THEN ADD ON.

DAD'S OLD FISHING HAT CAN SUPPORT AN EXPANDED BRIM OF CARDBOARD

① DAD'S OLD HAT

② CARDBOARD CUT AND GLUED TO THIS OLD HAT

④ CREATE THE FOCUS WITH EYES, NOSE

ADD EYES NOSE ETC.

FOAM STUFFING

① BASEBALL CAP

② AND EXPAND WITH CARDBOARD

③

FEET
MAKE TRIANGLE INTO CONES AND GLUE ONTO OLD TENNIS SHOES

② A MAD HATTER ①

① GLUE TOGETHER

FOAM HAT

②

OR JUST MAKE A SANDWICH

CUT OUT AND ASSEMBLE

HAIR

GLUE TOGETHER THE EDGES AND MAKE THE SANDWICH

② NO HAT NECESSARY ①

OR

EXPAND THE SANDWICH MASK INTO A WHOLE COSTUME

USE 3M #74 FOAM FAST ADHESIVE OR ALEENE'S THICK EXTRA TACKY GLUE

Origami Fold Foam Headpiece

MATERIALS

three-foot diamonds or squares of urethane
  foam

pins

3M #74 Foam Fast Adhesive

scissors

finishing materials as desired (spray can
  tops, bottle caps, paint, etc.)

Several of the steps you will take to make
this headpiece are the same as those in the
swan exercise you have just completed.
This time, however, the steps will be
applied to urethane foam. The headpiece
you make in this lesson will serve as a pro-
totype for many other foam constructions.

Decide whether the creature you are
planning to make would be constructed
best from a square shape of foam or from a
diamond. The look or orientation of your
headpiece will differ depending on which
shape you choose. A square will make a
tube-like headpiece in which the eyes
become the major focal point. When you
add the eyes to either shape you will begin
to see the basic character of your creature.

Once you have decided on a square or
diamond-shape approach, decide whether
the piece should fit over the head or on
the head. If you want to wear the piece on
your head, try rolling up the sides of the
headpiece and glue it in place. Pin the rear
to fit your head. If you want to wear the
piece over your head, glue together the
back edges leaving an opening through
which to insert your head.

1. To make an origami fold headpiece start
with a diamond-shaped piece of foam.
Create the nose by making a mountain-fold
and valley-fold at one end and fasten with a
clothespin. Repeat the fold to create two
eye sockets.

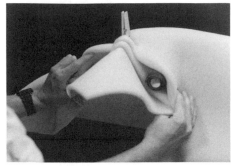

2. Spray can covers, film canisters, bottle
caps or similar found objects make dramatic
eyes. Glue the eyes into the sockets with
3M #74 Foam Fast Adhesive.

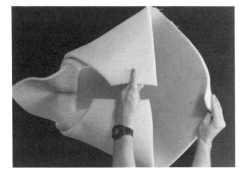

3. Bring the two sides and back together
like a fortune cookie.

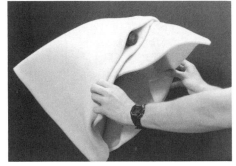

4. Remove clothespins and glue folds
with 3M #74 Foam Fast Adhesive.

5. Add piping (a folded over, glued foam
strip) for gums and details. Add teeth and
eyebrows made from scraps of foam.

6. Turn the headpiece hat over, roll up the
bottom edge and glue. This adjusts the
width for a better fit.

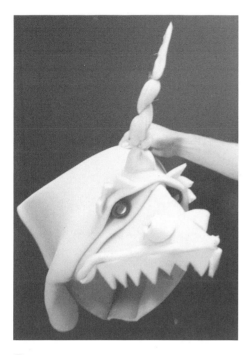

7. To make your headpiece a horned creature, start with a triangle of foam and make a narrow cone. Wrap and knot a string around the cone. Twist the horn to build more character. Tie off.

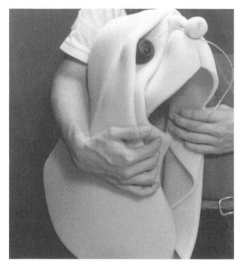

8. To make your headpiece a dog, fold under the front point of foam. Then fold the nose area in half, so the outside edges meet. Gather a bunch halfway up the fold and tie off the nose. Teeth, ears or other embellishments will add whatever personality you want your dog to have.

Working from a square gives your creature a different focus, while still using the same techniques.

creatures real and imagined

Animals have been a source of inspiration for artists throughout history. Examples of this can be found in the earliest cave paintings, the supernatural scarab and sphinx of ancient Egypt, gargoyles on Gothic churches, mythological beasts in paintings and sculpture and architecture of every era. For centuries animals have been important elements in heraldry and even today serve as patriotic symbols, as for example the American eagle and the British lion. The mythology, folklore and symbolism of every culture and area of the earth are intertwined with creatures either real or imagined.

We all interpret nature in our own ways. Whether a creature is real or imaginary, it can be portrayed in a real, imaginary, exaggerated or stylized manner. In the classroom one individual may be more visual or literary or mathematical than another, so the teacher needs to leave a sculpture's style optional for each child to develop in a personal way.

(Left) **Boris is an example of what you can do with carpet padding. Creatures like him figure strongly in Chinese traditions.**

Sources of inspiration for working with creatures are all around us. A search for sources can be an educational tool in itself. It can lead to a journey through the mythologies of many civilizations, providing a way to review our understanding of these societies.

Research pictures or videos of different animals from nature, mythology, legends and folklore.

For conceptual exercises, do some gesture drawings based on watching real animals in nature or on video. Try stylizing, abstracting or exaggerating parts. Experiment with wire sketches. Do some doodles and sketches on paper.

This chapter is concerned primarily with sculpture-in-the-round—sculpture to be viewed from all sides. There are three main parts to consider: the base, the armature and the body. The difference between working on a headpiece and a whole creature is mainly the addition of a base, or how the work is to be supported. Many of our creatures will be four-legged and lightweight. These might be freestanding. Larger pieces will probably need a distinct base for support. If a piece is to be suspended, a hanger must be an integral part of the design.

A Horse

MATERIALS

pencil
paper
aluminum clothesline
lighter wire
cotton string
plaster
burlap
wheat paste
water
newsprint
brown paper towels
water-soluble polyurethane

Research horses' proper body proportions and length of legs. As a conceptual exercise, practice doodling horses as a series of circles and gesture drawings. From these sketches you can establish your pose. Try to capture the pose in wire, using the same motion and volume as in the drawing.

A wire armature is adaptable for both papier-mâché and plaster. It can be used to build a form in detail or as an extension of a sketch, selectively developing some areas in detail and allowing some of the wire to remain exposed.

Aluminum clothesline is flexible and easy to use to form the large armature of a horse. Begin by bending an S curve of the backbone through the head. Wire four legs to the backbone via the shoulder and hip. For a plaster sculpture, rib cages and other details should be added with lighter wire. Tightly wrap the aluminum wire with cotton string to act as support for the plaster. Plaster-soaked burlap can be used to add bulk and develop the form. For

papier-mâché, a lighter wire armature can also be built around the backbone and legs. Fill out the form by adding crushed paper, keeping the sculpture lightweight. Add a skin and details such as a mane, tail or surface texture made from mâché-coated brown paper towel strips. A finish coat of water-soluble polyurethane provides a clear gloss.

Rolled and crushed paper on wire is an easy way to make most creatures. Horse by student Rachel Blackman.

Bamboo Piñata

MATERIALS

bamboo strips
lashes
newspaper or rolls of paper toweling
tape
wheat paste
water
paintbrush
several colors of tissue paper
scissors

Bamboo is a common armature for piñatas. Thin strips of bamboo have a linear strength and flexibility useful for bending in one direction. They are generally between one quarter- to three-eighths-inch wide and can be bowed, bent and tied to build a form. Bamboo shades found in import shops are a source of raw material.

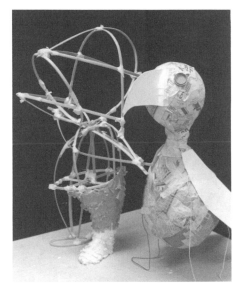

This partially disassembled piñata illustrates construction techniques.

Make an armature by tying together bamboo strips with tape or string. Wrap the figure with newspaper or paper towels (in rolls), and tape in place. Brush on wheat paste and begin adding layers of kraft paper and paste until you have covered the form. You only need a few layers, because the piñata is ultimately meant to be destroyed during party festivities.

After the papier-mâché is dry, cut strips of fringed tissue paper in bright colors and wrap them around the piñata to decorate. Balloons can be substituted for bamboo strips to build the form.

Traditionally, bamboo is used as an armature for piñatas in Mexico. Bamboo shades are a good source of supply.

Sculpted Paper Bull

MATERIALS

poster board
scissors
bull's horn
aluminum foil or paper toweling
newsprint
wheat paste
water
glue
surgical plaster gauze
paint and other finishing materials as desired

Do some conceptual paper-scoring exercises as a warm-up. Concentrate on simple scoring of lines and curves, notches and twists, because these are most useful for sculpting animals.

Paper sculpture techniques are particularly useful when used in conjunction with ready-made objects such as paper cups, oatmeal boxes and egg cartons. At times it is best to form your own shape for cutting and scoring, but make use of shapes already on hand whenever possible.

Using the sketches presented here as a reference, lay out and score a bull's skull and nose bridge. Cut and score two small pieces of poster board to enclose the ends of the skull and nose. Cut and score a half circle with slits on the edges to shape the cheeks. Use techniques from the conceptual paper-scoring exercises you did as a warm-up to form eyes, brows and nostrils.

There are two ways to make horns. The easiest way is to make lifts, or positive casts, from a real horn. If your family does not have a trophy room or den with mounted horns, try your local second hand shop or flea market. Cover the horn with aluminum foil or a layer of wet paper towels, then laminate strips of newsprint

dipped in wheat paste. When dry, remove the papier-mâché horn from the real one and tape it to the bull's head. Add a strip of mâché around the base of the horn to hold it in place. Repeat the process for the second horn.

If a real horn is not available, model one out of plasticene clay to cast from. Or cut two pieces of newsprint in the shape of a horn and glue them together along the long edges. Do not glue the bottom (short) edge. Cut flaps for attaching to the head. Stuff the horn to shape with more newsprint. When finished fold down the flaps and tape the horn to the sculpture.

Wads of paper or foil can be used to fill out the armature to the desired shape before applying papier-mâché or plaster surgical gauze. Paint or finish as desired.

The head may be used as a mask, wall hanging or trophy. To use it as a mask fit it to your face, taking care to locate the eyes of the mask. They can be inconspicuous holes for easy vision. Adding a frame and inserting a hanger is all the mask needs to function as a wall plaque. Make a trophy by adding the tapered end of a cone built up with papier-mâché to the bottom of the mask. Cut two crescent shapes of poster board that fit around the wide end of the cone. Score the crescents along their center lengths and glue them to an oval shape of cardboard cut to fit the base. Apply glue to the bottom edge of the cone and set it inside the raised crescents to complete the trophy's base.

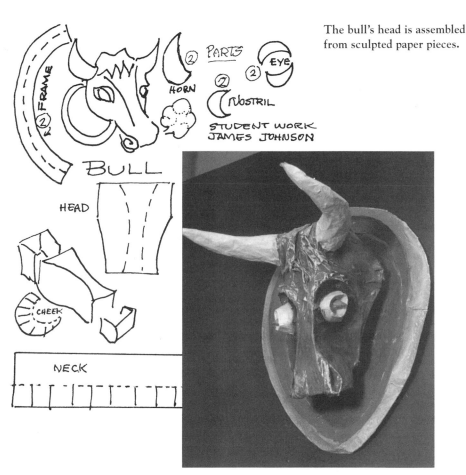

The bull's head is assembled from sculpted paper pieces.

Rolled Paper
Four-Legged Friend

MATERIALS

aluminum clothesline
newspaper
cylindrical rolls
paper cups
tape
paper towels
wheat paste
water
paint and finishing details as desired

Lay a piece of aluminum clothesline on a few sheets of newspaper and roll up to form a coil. Repeat, making two more coils. Use one coil to form the body and two for the legs, letting the size of the animal determine the length of each roll.

Adjust the contour of the coil to form the S curve of the backbone and neck. Bend the leg coils into V forms and tape to the backbone. Then bend the armature into the desired pose.

Add crushed paper to build up the form. Feel free to substitute bathroom tissue rolls, cups or whatever is available to fill out the form. A paper cup could become a nose, for example. Tape it all together.

Tear long strips of paper towels and wrap the armature to fully develop the creature's shape. Add newsprint papier-mâché strips, first to help support your wraps, then to become the body itself as the laminated layers dry. Paint and finish the sculpture as desired.

(Below) Three coils made from rolled paper over aluminum clothesline make an effective armature for four-legged creatures. Student Vanessa D'Sousa's cat armature catches the essential pose.

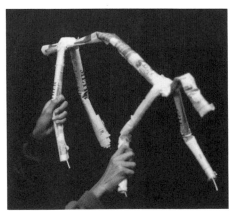

Template Creature

MATERIALS

cardboard or thin paneling material
corrugated paper
Elmer's SAF-T Contact Cement or 3M #30
    NF Contact Cement
kraft paper
wheat paste
white glue
water
finishing materials as desired
Optional: plaster, urethane foam

A simple silhouette of your creature is all you need. Cut a template of cardboard or thin paneling material and frame a base to hold it upright. Cut corrugated paper in 2" x 36" strips and coat them with Elmer's SAF-T Contact Cement or 3M #30 NF Contact Cement on both sides. Also paint the edges of the template where you want to build. Allow to dry for a half an hour or

until dry to the touch. Try to make your template round by building up a hollow shell of overlapping corrugated paper strips until your form is developed.

After the basic form is constructed, build it up with contact cement-coated kraft paper. Tear the coated paper into small pieces and build layer by layer until the surface is continuous and firm. The last layer should be kraft paper pasted with wheat paste, white glue and water for strength and water resistance. Finish as desired.

You may prefer to use plaster instead of papier-mâché to build your creature from the template stage. Using a urethane foam template is similar to working with one made of cardboard except that you stuff each side of the template under a sheet of foam that can be stretched or bloused to form the contours. Additional pieces of foam can be added after your basic shape is developed.

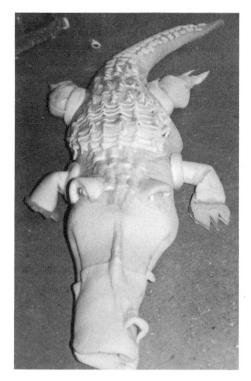

The template for a urethane foam alligator was stuffed. A top view of the gator was cut as a silhouette out of cardboard, and urethane foam scraps were piled on top. Then a slightly larger piece of foam was glued and stretched over like a skin.

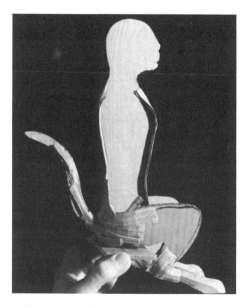

Advances in adhesives have made the template a valuable armature.

Sculptor Julian Strock uses contact papier-mâché to transform the template into a sculptured piece. After he completed the papier-mâché figure on the left, he covered it with plaster; the paper form became the armature.

A Friendly Balloon Dragon

MATERIALS

various size balloons
newsprint
wheat paste
water
paper towels
poster board
paper
Elmer's SAF-T Contact Cement
paint and other finishing materials
    as desired

The dragon can be a powerful stimulus for students' creativity. Dragons sometimes take the form of alligators, Gila monsters or lizards. Others appear as sea horses or armadillos, or even as the huge, mythical Pterodactylus birds of prehistoric times. From the study of mythology and history, we know that all civilizations have had their dragons. In folklore there is a difference between Eastern and Western hemisphere dragons. The Western dragon is very much the fire and brimstone image. He is fierce and breathes fire. On the other hand, the friendly Asian dragon protects cities and people.

Research the appearance of dragons throughout history in art and folklore. Spend some time doodling to come up with your own concept of a dragon. Once you have decided on a shape and size for your dragon, choose balloons to make up the bulk of the armature. You might select three balloons: one large one for the belly and two long segmented balloons, one for the neck and one for the tail. Cover with strips of papier-mâché. After the mâché dries remove the balloons, cut the mâché and reposition it to form the body.

Add crushed and scored paper to expand the forms. Make the head from a diamond-shaped piece of poster board folded in a single origami fold. Create a lower jaw from a triangle of poster board and paste it onto the head. Wings, legs and a firey tongue can all be made from scored and bent paper and poster board, then attached to the body with Elmer's SAF-T Contact Cement. Crumpled paper and paste-soaked paper towels may be used to fill out the form and add texture and details. Allow to dry, and paint and finish as desired.

Window Screen Bull

MATERIALS

aluminum clothesline
newspaper
window screen
plaster gauze
plaster
putty knife
file or carving tools
polymer medium
finishing materials as desired

Decide what pose you want your bull to assume. Sometimes quick gesture drawings are helpful in making your decision. Next, make a stick figure armature of aluminum clothesline and newspaper and bend it into its pose.

Cut a square of window screen and fold it over the stick figure armature. Stretch the screen until you have achieved the basic form you want your bull to take. Then wire it together with the loose ends of the screen. Cover the wire armature with a layer of plaster gauze. Mix only enough plaster for the project and build up the form with a putty knife. When the plaster has dried, file and carve the final shape. Add modeling paste for texture. Then coat with polymer medium and finish as desired.

Styrofoam Duck

MATERIALS

Styrofoam or insulation foam
Styrofoam cutter
Elmer's SAF-T Contact Cement
Surform rasp
sandpaper
fiberglass sheetrock tape
trowel
Dryvit Top Coat
scored paper
stain
beads and other finishing materials
    as desired
Options: papier-mâché, plaster, paint

A true sense of sculpting can be achieved by carving and shaping a single block of Styrofoam. If you have difficulty finding a block to work with, try laminating slabs together or use insulation foam as an alternative. To create a duck, cut eight pieces of Styrofoam or insulation foam into a silhouette of a duck and laminate them together with Elmer's SAF-T Contact Cement. Round out the shape with a Surform rasp, then use sandpaper to finish it. Cover the entire body with fiberglass sheetrock tape for strength and adhesion and trowel on a thin coat of Dryvit Top Coat for a super hard surface. Make stylized feathers from cut and scored paper, and glue them onto the body. A coat of stain applied to the entire surface, and then wiped off, will give your duck a sepia color. Add beads for eyes and other finishing details as desired.

Young sculptors may prefer to add texture and details made from papier-mâché or plaster instead of covering the duck with sheetrock tape and Dryvit Top Coat. A covering of papier-mâché or plaster can then be painted and finished as desired.

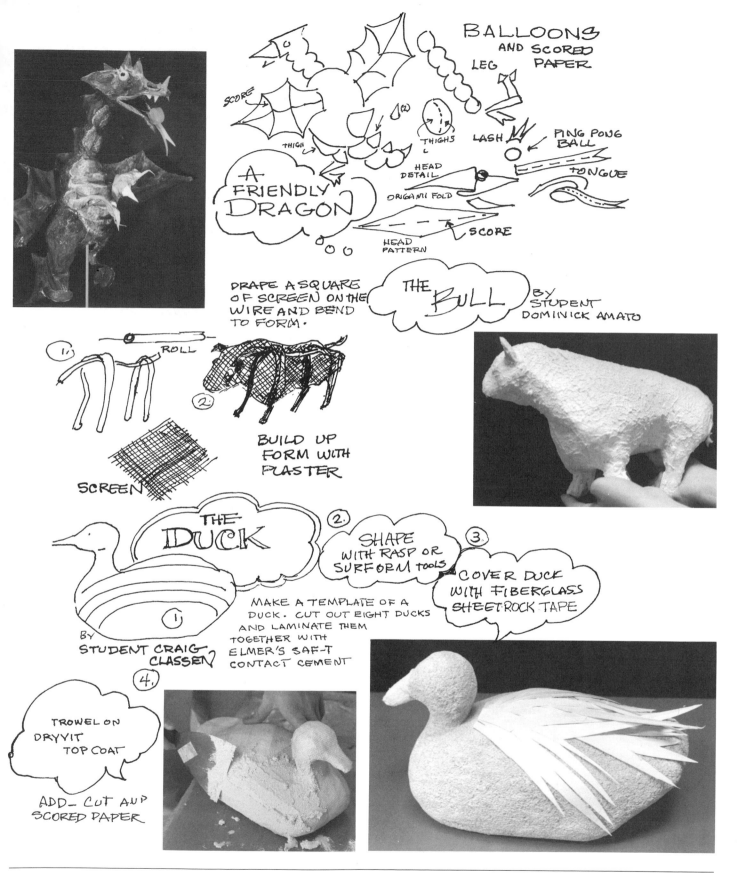

BALLOONS AND SCORED PAPER

LEG

SCORE

(2)

THIGHS

THIGH

A FRIENDLY DRAGON

HEAD DETAIL

ORIGAMI FOLD

LASH

PING PONG BALL

TONGUE

SCORE

HEAD PATTERN

O O

DRAPE A SQUARE OF SCREEN ON THE WIRE AND BEND TO FORM.

THE BULL BY STUDENT DOMINICK AMATO

1. ROLL

2.

SCREEN

BUILD UP FORM WITH PLASTER

THE DUCK

BY STUDENT CRAIG CLASSEN

1.

2. SHAPE WITH RASP OR SURFORM tools

3 COVER DUCK WITH FIBERGLASS SHEET·ROCK TAPE

MAKE A TEMPLATE OF A DUCK. CUT OUT EIGHT DUCKS AND LAMINATE THEM TOGETHER WITH ELMER'S SAF-T CONTACT CEMENT

4.

TROWEL ON DRYVIT TOP COAT

ADD— CUT AND SCORED PAPER

The Hydra

MATERIALS

backpack frame
flexible plastic pipe
hacksaw
duct tape
electric drill
twine
sheets of urethane foam
3M #74 Foam Fast Adhesive
found objects
aluminum clothesline
spray paint

The Hydra is a huge five-headed mythological creature that possesses the power to regenerate.

Begin with a backpack frame such as one left over from a hiking outing to serve as a support (the arm straps and belt are adjustable to fit different sizes).

You may also choose to construct a pack frame of plastic pipe. Use three-quarter-inch 200 PSI pipe (thin wall pipe) so that the pipe you will use for the Hydra's necks and wings can fit inside. If you have a ready-made frame, copy its dimensions. Cut half-inch CPVC pipe with a hacksaw for cross supports, and use duct tape to hold the frame together. Make sure it fits comfortably, then tie it together with twine for stability.

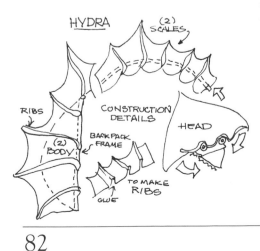

The next step is conceptual —planning how the necks will be arranged. This process can be almost like dancing. Warm up by doing a movement exercise, turning your body to the right while you imagine you are going to the left. This helps clarify space and determine the movement the necks will make with a person inside. Sketch the possibilities.

For the Hydra's curved necks, experiment with polyethylene pipe in three-quarters- to one-inch diameters to compare different characteristics (See Chapter Four, *Armatures*). Tie your rig on a chair and experiment with the pipes to make sure the creature is balanced. The two vertical pieces of the backpack frame should fit against your back while all the pieces of pipe for the heads should be lashed to the rear. For a taller sculpture, extend the vertical pieces of the frame by taping PVC pipe to them with duct tape.

The Hydra's skeleton is added to an ordinary backpack frame.

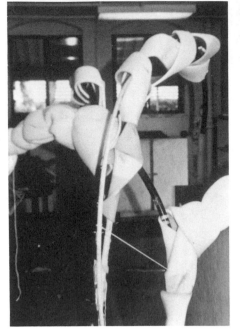

Foam sheet scraps are tied to the skeleton and are considered to be the stuffing necessary to add bulk.

Once you have finished experimenting and decided on your armature, drill holes in the pipes and pin them in place.

Add strips of scrap foam to the necks for stuffing, and loosely cover the necks with six-inch-diameter cylinders of foam. Knot a length of twine near the base of each neck and spiral it tightly around the neck to form a segmented esophagus.

Cut and add ribbed foam spires to the upper part of the necks. A rib adds strength and support just as a ribbed vault does in a cathedral. Notice how the necks hold their shapes.

Drape a sheet of foam over each side of the body for fit. The body should have more shape than the necks. Mark and cut serrations; fold ribs by gluing a fold at each point with 3M #74 Foam Fast Adhesive. Adhere each side of the body at the edges and adjoin opposite points of the spires.

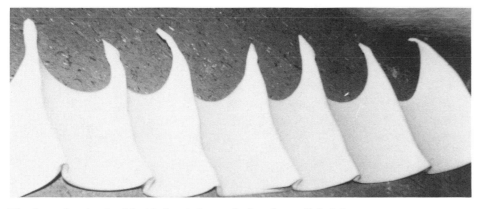

The foam sheeting is ribbed before it is attached to the stuffed skeleton.

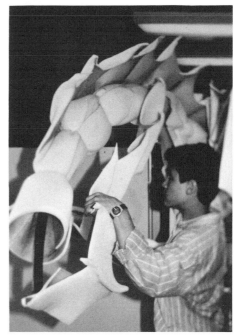

The dragon gains definition with the addition of an external skin. Glue the points of its back together before adding scales for the finished effect.

Heads are made from thirty-six-inch squares of foam. Start with a diamond shape, folding and gluing as in Japanese origami to form the snout, eye sockets, etc. Bring the two opposite points together to complete the head. For eyes choose a pair of found objects such as paint can lids, whiffle balls or Christmas ornaments.

Mount each head over a neck end and glue in place. Add details with scraps of foam. If a tongue is desired, use aluminum clothesline as support. You are now ready to paint. Plain white dragons make interesting sculptures, but aerosol spray paints are great for giving dragons color.

• SAFETY NOTE: Read spray paint directions carefully and use in a well-ventilated space. Spray enamel is not recommended for elementary school children. Teachers may prefer to use refillable aerosol spray cans with thin nontoxic acrylic paint as an alternative.

The Hydra can be easily animated with the wearer's hip movement and shifting weight. You can make the critter move without onlookers being aware of your actions since you are using a whip-like maneuver and actually moving in directions opposite from what is seen overhead.

The process of using a backpack as a frame for urethane foam sculpture can give birth to many species of dragons. Such projects also make it possible for students to interact with sculptural works from the inside as well as out. Issues of expression, proportion, balance and craftsmanship give this activity a personal connection between the object of art and the one who will wear it.

The Hydra turned out to be the greatest dragon of them all.

Seated Foam Gator

MATERIALS

1" x 2" pieces of wood cut to desired length for "T" bar

chicken wire

urethane foam

3M #74 Foam Fast Adhesive

old baseball cap

cardboard

found objects for details as desired

Optional: plywood or other suitable material for base

In the photo sequence that follows, you will see one way to create a foam creature using a "T" bar for support and chicken wire for an armature. With a little imagination, you can create a wide variety of creatures in any number of positions or poses by adapting the basic steps shown below to suit your purpose. If you choose a standing position for your creature, you must consider the base as an integral part of your design.

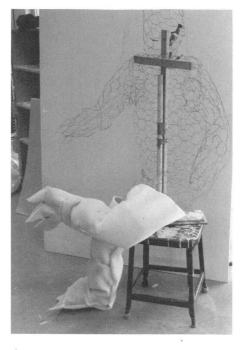

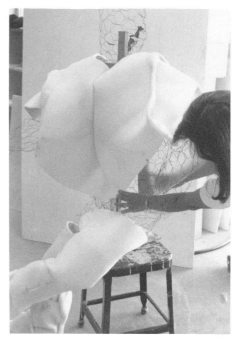

1. To make a foam gator using chicken wire armature, start with a tee frame on a base. The "T" bar acts as a hanger or support. In this case it is shortened because the figure will be seated. Construct cylinders of chicken wire and attach together section by section with wire to form the body armature.

2. Wrap sheets of urethane around the armature and glue together to form main parts of body.

3. Attach a piece of cardboard to the top of a baseball cap to form the nose and top jaw of the gator.

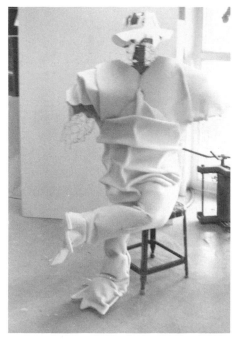

4. For the abdomen, cut a shape from foam and add ribbing for emphasis. Continue building your form section by section all the way down to the claws. Make the claws like three-finger gloves.

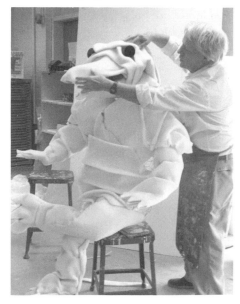

5. Cover your baseball hat armature with foam and add the triangle of foam for lower jaw. Complete the head details—lips, teeth and eyes from paint can caps or other found objects.

6. Cut two six-foot pieces of foam with matching spikes. Add a strip of glue across their widths at each spike and pinch the foam into ribs. Then glue the two halves together at the spike points. Position the full piece on the back of your gator starting at the head and secure with glue. Your gator now has a spiked back and tail.

EIGHT

puppets

Background

The puppet has been around for thousands of years. Artifacts of puppets have been found in archaeological digs in Egypt, Greece and Rome. The puppet show is one of the earliest forms of educational theater. Performances have been used to dramatize myths, legends and religious lessons. Bible stories were often told through the action of puppets during the Middle Ages to make them easier for the average person to comprehend.

The Italian tradition of puppetry known as the commedia dell'arte spread to England and gave rise to the famous *Punch and Judy* shows. Germany, Holland, Switzerland and Russia all developed their own similar versions. In the ancient Japanese theater form known as Bunraku, puppeteers dress in black and work in full view of the audience using rods to control four-foot-tall puppets. Religious lessons have traditionally been taught in India and China using shadow and rod puppets.

In modern times, United States audiences are more familiar with puppet heroes of radio and television. Famous puppets and puppeteers include Charlie McCarthy (1940s); Kukla, Fran and Ollie, and Howdy Doody (1950s); Captain Kangaroo (1960s and 1970s); and Shari Lewis (1960s to present). *Sesame Street*, starring the Muppets, has reinstitutionalized the puppet as a vital part of the educational scene today.

Generally there are five types of manually operated puppets, but the variations and combinations make it seem like many more. The five are hand puppets, rod puppets, marionettes, body puppets and larger-than-life puppets. In addition electronic technology has produced its own system to control puppets, although in many cases these are supplemented manually. The Muppets of *Sesame Street* now use electronics. The movie *Little Shop of Horrors* used electronically controlled puppets, while stage presentations often rely on traditional techniques and clever stagecraft for figure animation.

This chapter will concentrate on puppetry techniques most valuable for the classroom setting. Once students realize that the many types of finger puppets, glove puppets and mouth puppets are just variations of hand puppets, the mystery of puppetry will begin to unfold for them. While marionettes may at first seem to be in a class by themselves because they are operated by strings from above, students will find that their shows often include hand and rod puppets, too. The modern educational puppeteer uses everything at his or her disposal to explore the illusions of puppetry because, of course, the play is the thing.

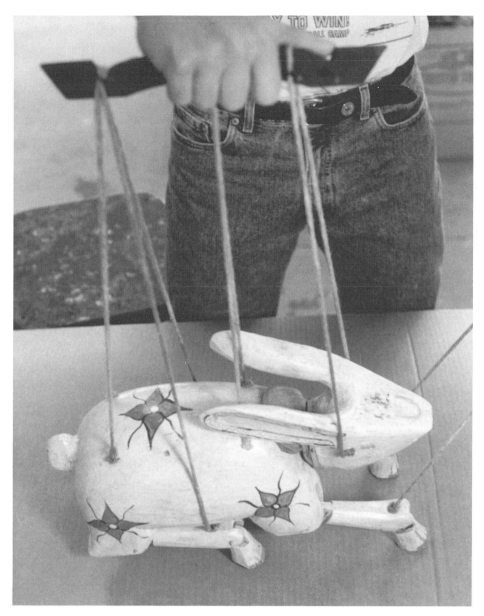

This antique rabbit is controlled by a bar and five ropes, which make him hop, jump, stretch, or do other rabbit-like things. Collection Catherine Wolfe.

Planning and Design

While great ideas sometimes appear to happen in a flash of inspiration, they are more often products of extensive brainstorming and making connections of trial and error. There is a big difference between an idea and a solution. A solution requires planning. The first step in planning a puppet project is to determine your overall concept for the puppet.

What is the puppet's purpose, education or entertainment? Will the puppet be small, large or larger than life? Need it be durable, or would a temporary puppet for limited use be more appropriate? Does it have to fly, dance or walk, or will it be a "talking head?"

Once you have answered these questions, you are ready to begin developing your design. Do some brainstorming, using any or all ideas. Research what has already been done in the art of puppetry. Don't try to re-invent the wheel.

It is a lot more economical to make sketches in search of an idea before you experiment with materials. The puppet show's story line will often determine the style of puppet design: real, imaginary, stylized or exaggerated. A lot of design decisions and fine-tuning will have to be made during construction, but unlike in human theater, the designer has complete control over the actors, so experimental approaches are possible.

Once you have a design, the search for materials can be critical for success. It is like going on a scavenger hunt—you have to believe in the magical possibilities of the seemingly unrelated collection of things you might come up with.

The Mitt Hand Puppet

MATERIALS

urethane foam
scissors
adhesive
paint
paintbrushes

The hands make wonderful puppets. Young children quickly discover that hands can "go walking" across bed sheets. With a little imagination, fingers can have faces and be made to talk to one another.

Hand puppet is a broad term meaning almost anything directly manipulated by the hand. Hand puppets are extremely versatile and the most widely used of all puppets. While their construction is simple and the control direct, hand puppets are also harder to move about because they are attached to your hands. They work easily for talking heads but are hard to move in diverse ways.

A simple mitt of urethane foam can be readily turned into two puppet characters by using each side of the mitt as a different character.

From a sheet of urethane foam, cut out two mitt shapes a little larger than your hand. Glue the edges together with adhesive, making sure there will be enough room for your hand inside.

• **SAFETY NOTE:** Choose an appropriate method of adhering fabrics depending on the age and skill of the workers (See Chapter Three, *Adhesives for Urethane Foam*).

Experiment with pieces of foam and other materials to fully develop the character of your puppet. Try the puppet on. Make it talk and act. See if it works.

Spray or brush colors on the foam either in sketch fashion or as solid areas.

Variation on a Mitt Hand Puppet

MATERIALS

crumpled newspaper
tape
soft drink bottle
strip or pulp papier-mâché
urethane foam
scissors
adhesive
paint
paintbrushes
other finishing materials as desired

This foam mitt puppet will have the distinction of a papier-mâché head. Make the head by wrapping and taping crumpled newspapers around the neck of a soft drink bottle. Build up details with either strip or pulp papier-mâché. When the mâché has dried remove the bottle and crumpled newspaper from the head. Paint and decorate the head to fit your character.

The mitt portion of this puppet is made the same way as described above and will become the costume for your character. Note, however, that the area normally dedicated to the head of the basic mitt puppet will have to be cut narrowly enough to fit into the neck of the papier-mâché head.

Mouth Puppet

MATERIALS

urethane foam
scissors
adhesives

This is a fancy dressed-up version of the old paper plate puppet you probably played with as a child.

Place your hand on a piece of foam and cut an oval larger than your hand. Using this as a pattern, cut another oval and cut it in half. Glue the edges of the half and whole ovals together. Open the ovals at the back and put four fingers in one and your thumb in the other. The uncut oval should be on the inside of your hand. This is your puppet base. For details, experiment with many pieces of foam or other materials to fully develop the character of your puppet. Cut pieces for the back, legs, or whatever other body parts and details you want. Try on your puppet. "Get inside" its head and make it talk and act.

For younger children, you might try making the puppets first, then letting the children wear them and get to know each other, finally letting them make up a story to fit the characters.

The Rod Puppet

The rod puppet offers more diversity of motion than the hand puppet, but at the cost of complexity. Rod puppets are controlled by homemade technology—a system of levers, springs, strings and rods which make the puppet talk and move its head, eyes and hands. The rods are usually visible but can sometimes be hidden in a large sleeve.

The head is attached to the end of a rod which slides through the neck of the puppet body, making it possible to turn the head while the body remains still. A nodding up-and-down movement can be controlled with a lever on the stick which is connected to a rod that moves the head. If desired, additional movements can be added to the main rod controls to roll the eyes open and closed.

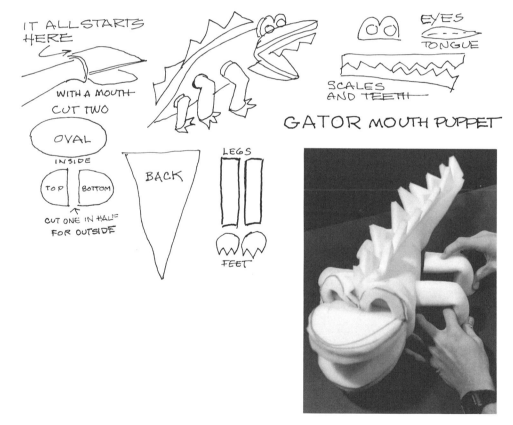

IT ALL STARTS HERE

WITH A MOUTH

CUT TWO

OVAL

INSIDE

TOP   BOTTOM

CUT ONE IN HALF FOR OUTSIDE

BACK

LEGS

FEET

EYES

TONGUE

SCALES AND TEETH

GATOR MOUTH PUPPET

Puppeteer Harry Mayronne, Jr. operates rod puppet Miss Viola by turning a rod that connects to the head, while moving the arms with a stick.

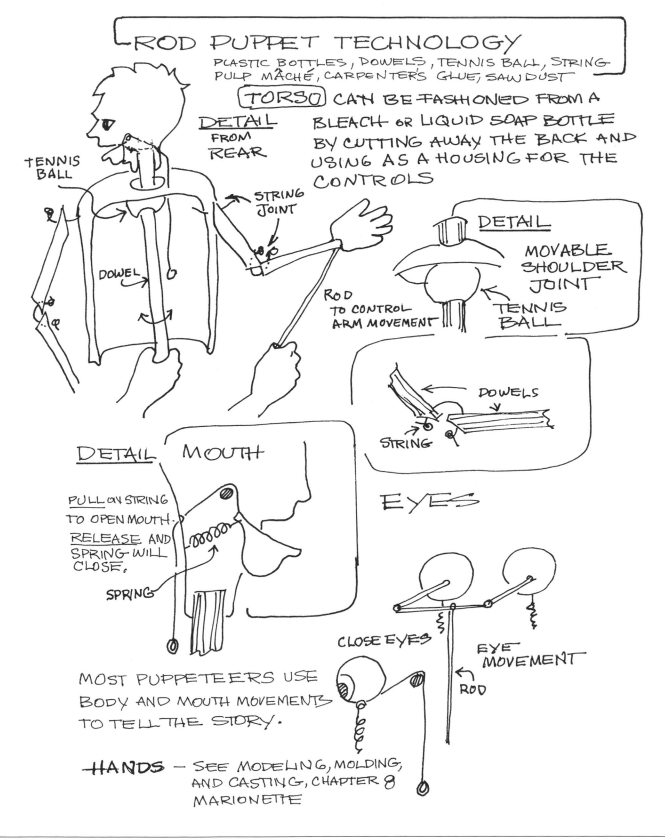

ROD PUPPET TECHNOLOGY

PLASTIC BOTTLES, DOWELS, TENNIS BALL, STRING
PULP MÂCHÉ, CARPENTER'S GLUE, SAWDUST

TORSO CAN BE FASHIONED FROM A BLEACH OR LIQUID SOAP BOTTLE BY CUTTING AWAY THE BACK AND USING AS A HOUSING FOR THE CONTROLS

DETAIL FROM REAR

TENNIS BALL

STRING JOINT

DOWEL

ROD TO CONTROL ARM MOVEMENT

DETAIL MOVABLE SHOULDER JOINT

TENNIS BALL

DOWELS

STRING

DETAIL MOUTH

PULL ON STRING TO OPEN MOUTH.
RELEASE AND SPRING WILL CLOSE.

SPRING

EYES

CLOSE EYES

EYE MOVEMENT

ROD

MOST PUPPETEERS USE BODY AND MOUTH MOVEMENTS TO TELL THE STORY.

HANDS — SEE MODELING, MOLDING, AND CASTING, CHAPTER 8 MARIONETTE

This method of indirect control makes it possible to operate the puppet from a stand attached to a stage railing, freeing the puppeteer for other action.

A close study of Rod Puppet Technology on the previous page should be enough to start the do-it-yourselfer on a journey of puppet engineering. Heads and body parts can be made from papier-mâché, plaster or foam. Sticks and rods are used with all size puppets. The huge Bread and Puppet figures are manipulated with long rods. The Japanese Bunraku are controlled by rods as are the shadow puppets of India.

Building the Head

The head of a rod puppet can be made in a number of ways. It can be carved in Styrofoam; modeled in crushed aluminum foil and covered with plaster gauze or papier-

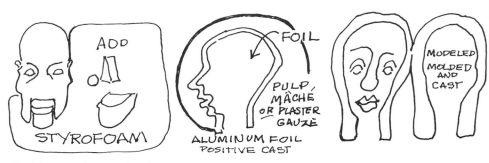

Building a rod puppet head.

mâché; or modeled in clay, molded in plaster and cast in papier-mâché. The lessons below will describe how to build the head from Styrofoam and aluminum foil. For information about modeling, molding and casting heads refer to the Marionettes section later in this chapter.

Styrofoam Head

MATERIALS

Styrofoam
hacksaw blade
serrated paring knife
sandpaper
fabric
paper
white glue
Elmer's SAF-T Contact Cement
paint

Start by deciding what type of character your puppet will assume, using quick gesture drawings as needed to generate ideas. The head itself can be carved from a Styrofoam ball or other form with a hacksaw blade or serrated paring knife, then refined with sandpaper.

• **SAFETY NOTE:** Students using knives and other sharp carving tools must be

closely supervised. Sharp tools are not recommended for use by young children.

Any pieces you may cut from the head can be glued on in a different spot with Elmer's SAF-T Contact Cement, and shaped and sanded as facial features to finish. Next, cover the head with papier- or fabric mâché. Either of these will add durability to the head. Paint or finish the head to suit your character.

If solid Styrofoam is not available, cut and laminate pieces of insulation foam together as an alternative.

Aluminum Foil Head

MATERIALS

aluminum foil
pulp mâché
white glue
plaster gauze
paper
paint

Once you have established your character, aluminum foil can be crumpled and shaped to form the armature for your head. Cover the armature with pulp or strip mâché, or plaster gauze. Build up facial features and finish as desired.

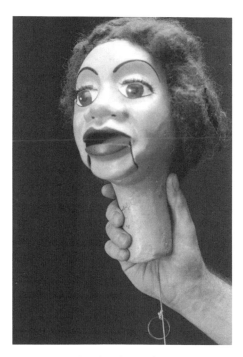

Miss Viola's head and mouth are controlled by a wire ring located behind her head. This ring opens and closes the mouth.

Marionettes

Marionettes are often thought of as the most complicated kind of puppet, with formal systems of strings controlled by puppeteers above the stage. Actually, marionettes range from the very simple to the complex. A handkerchief, sock, rubber band and a few strings are all that is needed to create a dancing marionette. While most marionettes resemble people or animals, some are gadgets or utensils animated by strings. As with all puppets, the only limitation on the form and substance of the marionette is the imagination of the maker.

The Anatomy of a Traditional Marionette

The number of parts of the marionette body will depend on the amount of reality or expressiveness desired. Many puppets are made in eleven pieces, with hands and feet part of the lower arms and legs. When hand and foot gestures are consid-

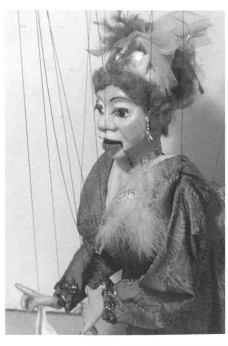

Miss Viola as a marionette on stage.

(*Below*) Miss Viola's rigging is a system of strings tied between moveable crossbars, or the *airplane*, and her arms, legs and other moveable parts. Courtesy Harry Mayronne, Jr., puppet maker.

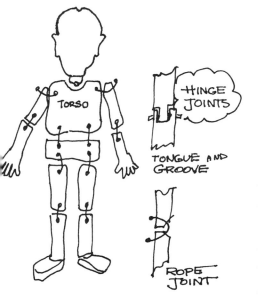

Diagram of the traditional marionette's moving parts and joints.

ered important parts of a puppet's personality, the marionette can be constructed so the appendages are manipulated separately.

Most of the puppet's moving parts can be connected with rope or hooks and eyes, but the two parts of the arms and legs should be jointed in some way so they approximate the movement of the human body. A tongue-and-groove joint can be effective in producing a realistic puppet, but it does require some skill to make. An effective substitute is the rope joint.

The head of a marionette should be exaggerated because an audience's normal viewing distance from a puppet obscures small details. Often expressive details such as eyes should be enlarged to provide a focus for the audience.

Building the Body

Many different materials can be used to make body parts. Traditional puppets like Pinocchio are made of wood, but an imaginative artist might use anything that works, including papier-mâché, aluminum foil, plasticene clay, salt dough, wood filler, Styrofoam, chicken wire, urethane foam or a mixture of media. Wood, clay, papier-mâché and Styrofoam are best used for the head, hands and feet, while wood alone is still the easiest and most popular material for the body.

The torso and pelvis are cut from a 1" x 2" or 1" x 3" piece of wood. Wooden dowels make effective arms and legs and are readily available at hardware stores. One-inch sticks may substitute dowels if necessary. For best results, the dowels or sticks should be tapered to fit a hinged joint. Hands and feet can be modeled in clay, carved in Styrofoam or molded and cast in papier-mâché or other appropriate material. They can be permanently attached to the limbs or hinged if the puppet must do more complex movements.

Controls and Rigging

The best way to begin is to start simply. Begin with a cross and see how it works.

The "Airplane" is appropriately named since it looks like an airplane.

This is a sample string rigging for an "Airplane" horizontal control.

Legs. A removable wing can fly free or be stationed at the dowel until needed for making the puppet run and jump.

Head. The eyes on the head are attached to the end of the "cross," or main wing.

Hands. A sliding string is attached to the eye on the nose of the plane.

Shoulders. A continuous string loops through two eyes in the midsection of the plane body and connects to the shoulders.

Back. A tail string attaches to the bottom of the back for bowing.

Marionette with Cast Head

MATERIALS

sketch paper
pencil
plasticene clay
string
separator
casting material (plaster, strip papier-mâché, papier-mâché mash, plastic wood, salt dough or wood filler)
paint and finishing materials as desired
marionette body and rigging

Plasticene modeling clay is a favorite of many puppet makers, especially where detail is important.

Begin the modeling process by sketching the head you want for your marionette at the actual size needed. Model an egg shape in plasticene and divide it into thirds: hairline to eyebrows, brows to nose tip and nose tip to chin. Model the marionette's features and add texture. Add a rounded neck to fit the body.

Next, make a mold from the model. To make a two-piece negative mold, you must start with a cardboard box or build a wooden frame deep enough to hold the plasticene model with at least two inches to spare. Cover the inside of the box or frame with plastic sheeting and allow the plastic to overlap all four sides.

Mix enough plaster for the bottom half of the mold and fill the box halfway. Pour the plaster slowly to avoid creating air bubbles. When the plaster begins to set, lower the model into it halfway and hold the model until the plaster is firm. When the plaster is completely dry, cut two notches into it as a guide for aligning the top half of the mold. Do not remove the model.

Spread petroleum jelly on the top edge of the mold. Mix and pour enough plaster for the top half of the mold. The plaster should now fill the box.

After the plaster is completely dry, pry the mold open and remove the model. Coat the inside of your mold with a separator and you are ready to cast.

Casts can be made in plaster, strip papier-mâché, papier-mâché mash, homemade plastic wood (white glue and sawdust) or salt dough. Remember, the cast must be hollow if you plan to use controls in the

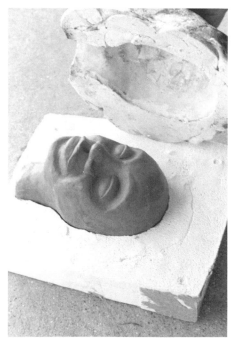

A mold can be used many times to make multiple heads. Courtesy Harry Mayronne, Jr.

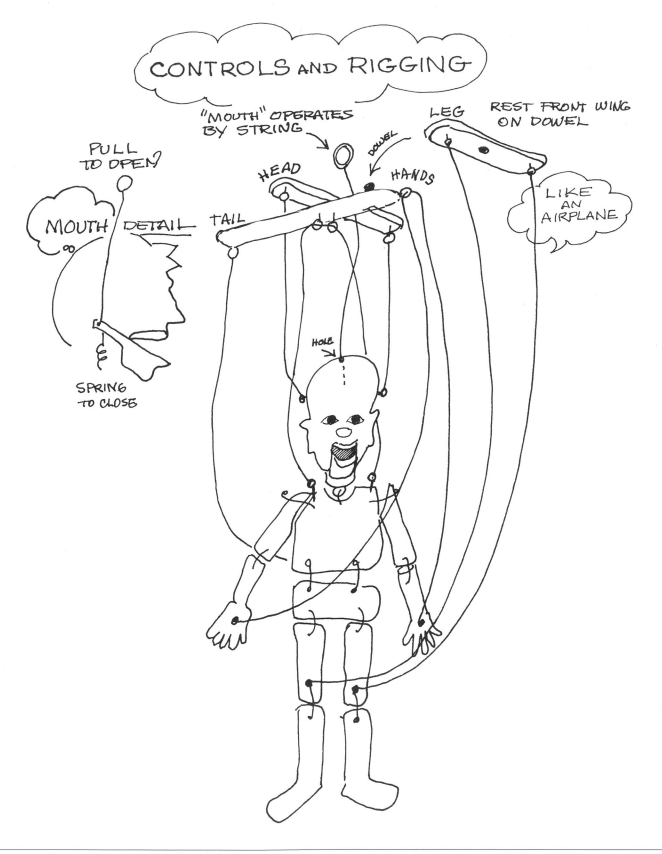

CONTROLS AND RIGGING

"MOUTH" OPERATES BY STRING

PULL TO OPEN?

MOUTH DETAIL

HEAD

DOWEL

HANDS

TAIL

LEG

REST FRONT WING ON DOWEL

LIKE AN AIRPLANE

SPRING TO CLOSE

HOLE

head. Layer or pack your cast material into the mold until it is one-quarter inch thick in each half of the mold. Tie the two halves together if you are casting a one-piece head. Allow the cast to dry completely, then remove it from the mold. Fasten the two halves together if you have cast the head as separate pieces.

Allow the head to dry. Paint and decorate as desired, and attach to marionette body and rigging.

Marionette with Styrofoam Head

MATERIALS

Styrofoam

Elmer's SAF-T Contact Cement

carving tools such as knives, rasps, hacksaw blade or Styrofoam cutter

marionette body and rigging

Build up a marionette head by gluing pieces of Styrofoam together with a non-toxic contact cement such as Elmer's SAF-T Contact Cement, and then shape as desired.

•SAFETY NOTE: Students using knives and other sharp carving tools must be closely supervised. Sharp tools are not recommended for use by young children.

After carving, cover the head with cloth, papier-mâché or other material to protect it from abrasions.

Paint and decorate as desired, and attach to a marionette body and rigging.

Life-Size Marionette

MATERIALS

one-piece footed baby pajamas

crumpled paper or foam scraps

needle

thread

plaster gauze

Styrofoam head

pair of mittens

shoes or weights

clothing or other finishing decorations as desired

rigging materials

Life-size puppets can be made quickly from one-piece baby pajamas with feet. Stuff

Stuff one-piece footed baby pajamas to create a life-size marionette.

the pajamas with crumpled paper or foam scraps and sew sections together as indicated on the diagram.

Use a Styrofoam head with a plaster gauze cast face as the marionette's head and mittens stuffed with foam for the hands. Either put on shoes or add weights to the feet, and you are ready for decorating, dressing and rigging.

An adult-size marionette could be made out of a mechanic's jumpsuit.

Body Puppets

Traditional puppetry has been expanded to life-size and even larger constructions. The colossal Big Bird of *Sesame Street*, the creatures of *Where the Wild Things Are* and the carnivorous Audrey II of *Little Shop of Horrors* are examples of large-scale puppets in action.

Technology has expanded the potential of this form of puppet. The actor inside the "skin" of a puppet might be in charge of the movement while a remote puppeteer controls the eyes and mouth movement and voice electronically.

With a little ingenuity, a wide range of puppet actions can be engineered in the classroom without advanced technology. A few strings and a flexible armature can put the body puppet under total control of the wearer. The rod puppet offers a key to some of the solutions.

The Swamp Creature

MATERIALS

large sheets of cardboard
scissors
large sheets of urethane foam
aluminum clothesline
adhesive
balls for eyes (tennis balls, Christmas balls, spray can covers)
spray paint

This body puppet is designed in two parts, head and body. The enlarged head provides the upper jaw while the body contains the lower jaw.

Head. A cardboard rectangle in a C shape with a hole for the head is the armature for a swamp creature head. A constructed helmet can be mounted inside to hold the creature's head in position while wearing.

Body. Cut a collar of cardboard, score and fold it into a breastplate. Wrap a piece of urethane foam about the wearer's body forming a cylinder. There should be enough foam at the top to cover the collar. Adhere the foam to the collar and cut arm holes. Thread two pieces of single-strand aluminum clothesline to the breastplate, creating the armature for the lower jaw.

Drape, fold and glue a big square of urethane foam to the head armature and loosely form the shape of the head. Drape and tuck the foam for maximum three-dimensional effect. Add ribs and points as desired, and build a dramatic tail. Cut two pieces of foam for the tail, one for each side.

Cover the lower jaw armature with a large square of foam, and glue and shape to form the lower jaw.

Now for the all-important details.

The eyes can be as important to a swamp creature as they are to a person. Tennis balls, Christmas tree balls or spray can covers all make exciting eyes. Use half circles of foam for each eyelid. Add lashes and other details for emphasis.

Cut triangles of foam and glue into cones for teeth located on the upper and lower jaws.

Cut long strips of foam about two inches wide and up to six feet long. Fold and glue lengthwise to create gums and lips. Let the strips outline the gum line, making sure to outline the bases of teeth as you go.

Spray the body with circular motions to stimulate scales or a crusty skin.

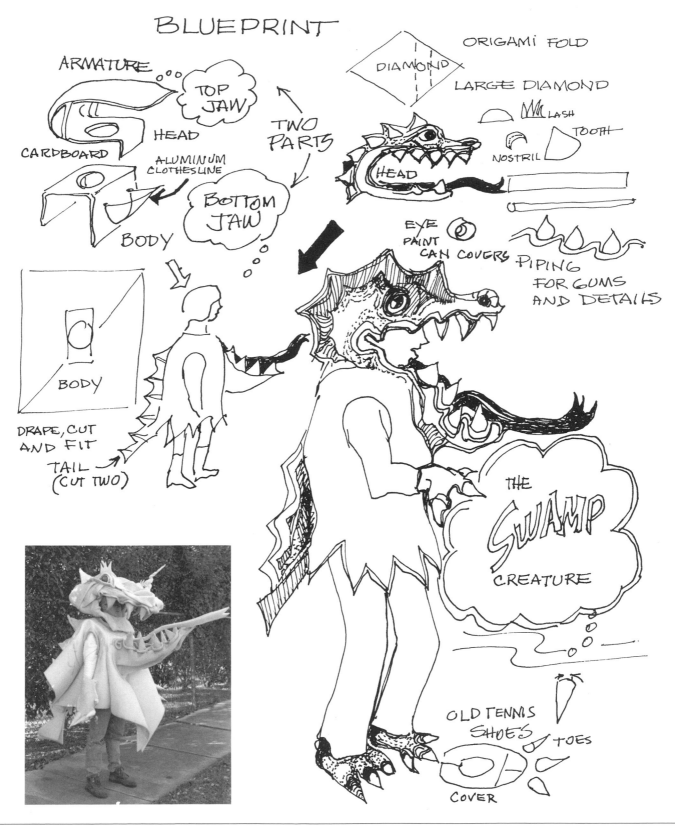

BLUEPRINT

ARMATURE

TOP JAW

HEAD

CARDBOARD

ALUMINUM CLOTHESLINE

BOTTOM JAW

BODY

TWO PARTS

ORIGAMI FOLD

DIAMOND

LARGE DIAMOND

LASH

HEAD

NOSTRIL

TOOTH

EYE
PAINT
CAN COVERS

PIPING
FOR GUMS
AND DETAILS

BODY

DRAPE, CUT
AND FIT

TAIL
(CUT TWO)

THE
SWAMP
CREATURE

OLD TENNIS
SHOES

TOES

COVER

(*Opposite*) **Blueprint for the swamp creature.**

Continue this detailing on both jaws. Add extra drool made from thin strips of foam if desired.

If this is a fire-breathing creature, cut two identical three-inch jagged flame-like strips three feet long. Add a tongue. Mount on the cardboard breastplate and point forward—to scare off evil spirits.

Now you are ready to paint. There are many ways to paint your creature, but the use of spray paint will be discussed here.

Begin with light colors before dark ones and don't be afraid to leave white space. Next paint the lips, teeth and other details. Spray the body with circular motions to simulate scales or crusty skin. Repeat with a darker color. Add details last. Try to create a focus or center of interest.

Spray the paint with a glancing stroke, a stroke at a 45° angle, to get a shaded effect, or go in close to establish a bright detail line. Blend colors by overlapping glancing strokes.

•SAFETY NOTE: Always wear a respirator or face mask and work in a well-ventilated space when using spray paint. Young children should not use spray paints. Students in upper grade levels should be supervised closely during use.

the human figure

Sculptural styles of portraying the human figure have alternated from real to imaginary and from exaggerated to stylized in cycles throughout history. The human figure in the kingdoms of ancient Egypt was meant to be viewed from the front. Sculpted figures were usually designed from cubes. Hellenistic, or ancient Greek and Roman, sculpture was based on the cylinder and conceived in the round, to be viewed from all sides. The Greeks and the Romans also added the action pose. In the Middle Ages figures on portals of Gothic cathedrals were elongated and exaggerated. Gargoyles on the roof of the Cathedral at Chartres were supposed to scare off the devil. The twentieth century brought on the bimorphic forms of Henry Moore. His "Swiss cheese" look opened up a new element in figure sculpture, the void, or empty space.

The human figure can be carved from a solid, built up on an armature, cast from a mold or cast from the body itself. It can be created using different armatures and media, such as wire, cardboard, chicken wire, papier-mâché, plaster, foam and mixed media. The possibilities for finishes, colors and patinas are virtually limitless (See Chapter Two).

The classical concept of proportioning a figure's height as seven-and-a-half times the length of the head is still used as a basis of perfection, although the average person's body today is more like eight-and-a-half times the head.

Planning and Design Steps

Begin any lesson in sculpting the human figure with some conceptual exercises. Sketch figures quickly in different poses. Do some gesture or contour drawings or wire sketches.

Research how the human body looks in different poses and movements. Make a book of pictures from magazines and newspapers showing the human figure in different activities. Collect photos of everyday life, sports, dance and theater.

(Opposite) Duane Hanson's *Bus Stop Lady.* Hanson makes life casts from snapshots of ordinary blue collar people doing ordinary things. K + B Plaza, New Orleans, Louisiana. Courtesy Virlane Foundation.

(Below) Henry Moore's *Reclining Mother with Child* demonstrates the use of empty space in this recurring theme of mother and child. K + B Plaza, New Orleans, Louisiana. Courtesy Virlane Foundation.

Wire Armature Figure

MATERIALS

large pieces of paper
pencil
aluminum clothesline
masking tape
cotton string
wire screen
plaster or papier-mâché
sandpaper
carving tools
finishing materials

Experiment with different poses. Use the armature to find the pose you want.

The aluminum clothesline armature is the easiest way to learn about sculpting the human figure. Lay out the proportions of a figure on a large piece of paper. Divide the body into three equal parts minus the head: shoulder to hip, hip to knee, knee to foot. Add the head.

Trace the sketch with three pieces of aluminum clothesline, one for the head, backbone and left leg; one for the right leg and hip; and one for the arms and shoulders. Tape the connections as indicated, then bind them with string.

Bend your figure to different poses, intuitively discovering the pose you want to sculpt in the process. This might be the *contrapposto*, or classical Greek pose in which the hips and shoulders are placed assymetrically opposite each other on the central axis of the spine and the weight of the figure is shifted to one leg. Choose a figure at rest, sitting, running, walking or taking part in some other action.

Now that your figure has discovered its pose, the next step is constructing the support or base. If the figure is standing, it might be nailed to a wooden base. If leaping or dancing, it might be anchored in a cup of plaster. A jumping or flying figure will probably need an independent support, while a reclining, resting or sitting figure might need none at all. In any case, the design of the support or base is an integral part of the design and needs as much care as the figure itself.

Once the basic wire armature is completed, it can be covered with either papier-mâché or plaster. Wire screen and other filler may be added before building up the form. If using plaster, add it slowly, mixing small amounts at a time. Continue to build until the shape is formed. File it with a rasp when hard and dry, then sand and finish with stains, patinas or colors (See Chapter Two, *Plaster*).

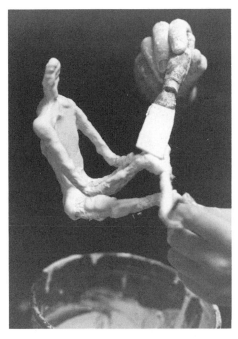

Add plaster to slowly build up form.

This sculpture of children at play is a composition of many figures in a group. Papier-mâché on a wire armature.

Slotted Cardboard Figure

MATERIALS

sheets of cardboard

scissors

utility knife

Elmer's SAF-T or 3M #30 NF Contact
    Cement

kraft paper

duct tape

white glue

Cardboard offers a simple and often free medium for sculpting the human figure.

Slotted cardboard sculpture simply involves putting together pieces of cardboard with interlocking slots. It produces an effective armature for papier-mâché or foam. This armature can be used for papier-mâché as is or built up using the contact mâché technique.

In contact papier-mâché, corrugated paper can be used to build the form directly.

Coat the corrugated paper and the template with Elmer's SAF-T Contact Cement or 3M #30 NF Contact Cement. Let dry for approximately one-half hour. When dry, cut it into strips and build the figure using the slotted cardboard armature as a base. Once again, the form can be finished with kraft paper and glue or with partially exposed corrugated texture.

Cardboard Template Figure. The cardboard template is simply a silhouette of the figure to be sculpted that is supported by a base. It works the same way as slotted cardboard except that the template armature is not as multidirectional. The template can also be used as part of a slotted cardboard armature. It is the most practical armature for most contact mâché work.

Both the slotted cardboard armature and the template are adaptable to urethane foam. The armature can be stuffed and sheathed to create your figure using techniques from previous chapters.

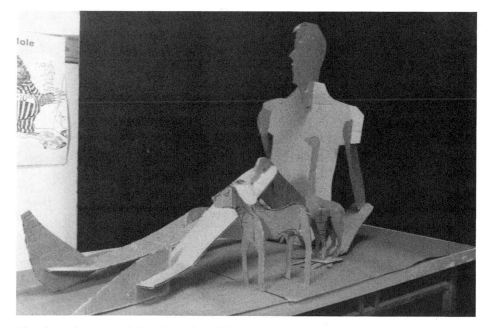

The three-dimensional slotted cardboard figure "expands" the potential of a two-dimensional template or can be a sculpture by itself.

Chicken Wire Figure

MATERIALS

1" x 2" strips of wood

handsaw

nails

plywood

chicken wire

tin snips

paper towels

tape

newsprint

wheat paste

water

kraft paper

latex paint

water-based polyurethane

Optional: urethane foam, 3M #74 Foam
    Fast Adhesive, plaster gauze, white glue,
    muslin

Before you begin working with chicken wire, you must build a support or stand. If the figure is to be upright, a "T" bar of 1" x 2" wood strips anchored to a base is an easy way to hang your piece while you are building and may become a permanent part of the armature for support.

Cut a piece of 1" x 2" wood a little longer than your figure. Nail a crosspiece for the shoulders. To hold the figure erect, add a base of plywood that can be shortened depending on the figure's final pose or replaced with a more permanent one when the sculpture is finished.

Cut and make cylinders of chicken wire following the simplified proportions illustrated on page 102.

Begin with the chest and follow with the legs, then the arms and finally the head. Wire the parts to one another with the loose ends of the chicken wire. Shape

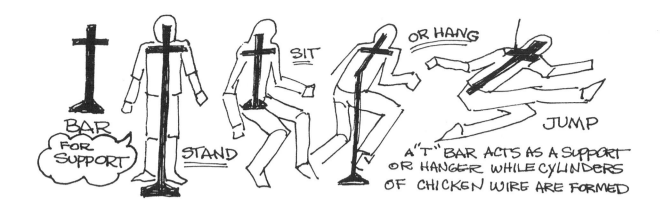

BAR FOR SUPPORT

STAND

SIT

OR HANG

JUMP

A "T" BAR ACTS AS A SUPPORT OR HANGER WHILE CYLINDERS OF CHICKEN WIRE ARE FORMED

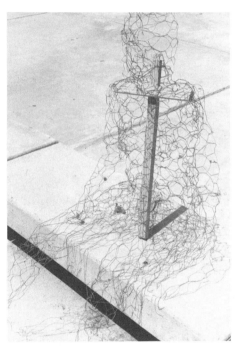

A seated figure armature is ready for papier-mâché application.

the hands and feet as triangles and wire into place. Chicken wire can easily cut and scratch your hands, so care must be taken when handling the loose ends.

Roll dry paper toweling around the chicken wire form until you have covered one area of the sculpture, then tape it in place. Continue until you have covered a major portion of your figure like a mummy. Before going any further, layer large strips of newsprint papier-mâché over the form like a wet skin. Once you have completed the first portion, resume rolling toweling around other portions until you have covered your figure once with a coat of toweling and pasted strips. Drying time may be needed at intervals depending on the size of your form. Continue laminating layers, alternating kraft paper with newsprint for the last layers until desired thickness is attained.

Another way to make the form quickly is to cover the chicken wire with urethane foam and tape it into place. The foam evens out the armature's surface before proceeding. Use the foam with its reverse side—the one with the skin—out. Cut, stretch, tape and glue (3M #74 Foam Fast Adhesive) in place until a skin covers the wire. Then begin the papier-mâché. This technique also works for creating a plaster gauze figure.

For more detail, feet, hands and the face can be cast in plaster gauze from a model, then attached to your papier-mâché figure. Laminate your last layer of mâché by adding white glue to the wheat paste or water for a hard surface and more support.

You may opt to cover your chicken wire armature with plaster-soaked muslin rather than papier-mâché, but plaster fabrication is much heavier than papier-mâché and requires substantially strengthened supports and base.

A coat of light-colored latex paint will smooth the figure's surface before any decorative painting. Use water-based polyurethane for a clear finish coat.

The Head in Relief

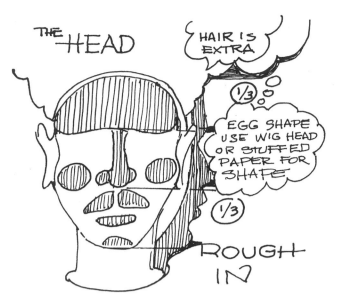

MATERIALS

paper
pencil
plasticene clay
sharp stick
box or wooden frame
plaster
petroleum jelly

No one phase in the life of an aspiring art student is more fear-inspiring than the first encounter with modeling a head. Students often forget where features belong, and the mouth rarely has room for teeth.

To overcome this problem, begin your sculpture lesson with some conceptual exercises. Sketch the head from different views and with different light sources. Research the structure of the skull and

Relief: Turkish slave girl. Early work by author at age sixteen.

muscles around the head. Have students observe themselves in the mirror. Observe the heads on coins and medallions.

Form a flat slab of plasticene clay about one-half inch thick as a base. Draw an outline of your relief head with a pencil or sharp stick. Build up the face to simulate three dimensions, much like a coin or cameo. More depth in the clay produces higher relief in the sculpture. Shallow relief is called *bas-relief*.

Individual heads look different, but this simple layout can be used as a general guide. Divide the head (minus hair) into three parts, hairline to brow to nose tip to chin. Align the ears with the middle third—the brow to the nose tip.

It is important to note that the skull extends above the hairline. An oversight in this area creates a Neanderthal man. You must add the hair to make this system work. Even if you plan to make a bald

figure you must still consider the hairline issue when constructing the head.

Technically, the most difficult part of a relief is the setting of the eyes and mouth. Close your eyes and feel your own a number of times before trying to form them in clay. The mouth may seem easy, but remember that there are teeth inside which must be allowed for.

Check your plasticene head for any undesirable undercuts. Then prepare your box or wooden frame as described in the Marionette with Cast Head lesson (page 94) and continue on with those instructions to create a plaster mold of your plasticene head. When the plaster is dry, remove the model and coat the inside of the mold with petroleum jelly. You are now ready to cast.

The Head–in–the–Round

MATERIALS

Styrofoam wig head or taped crushed paper

plasticene clay

metal shims or strips cut from a manilla file folder

petroleum jelly or liquid soap

plaster

bluing

string

materials for finishing as desired

Start with a Styrofoam wig head or taped crushed paper as a ready-made armature. Cover the whole head with a thin layer of plasticene clay. Divide the head vertically into thirds to lay out the proportions. Rough in the features according to your layout. Add a large patty of clay to the dome and a substantial amount to the forehead area. Attach a triangular wedge to the face. The nostrils can be carved in the cast later. Dig out the eye sockets and add eyeballs and lids. If you are uncertain about contours, use your face as a model and try to work by feeling your own features. Feel your mouth again and build out the sculpture's mouth to account for teeth. Rough in the ear as a C shape and locate it according to the diagram. Add small coils to simulate the hair pattern.

When the rough sculpture is complete, you are ready for details. Always proceed by adding or subtracting small amounts of clay, and don't be afraid to change the whole area if it doesn't work.

Before you call your head finished, make sure it is truly a sculpture-in-the-round, ready to be viewed from all angles. The back and sides should be as exciting as the front. Try to eliminate any undercut which would prevent easy removal of the head from a mold.

First, cover the Styrofoam head with plasticene. Then rough in the forehead, nose, cheeks, mouth and chin. Student work by Sophia Strata.

Finish building the form and add details, such as ears and hair. Student work by Sophia Strata.

Consult Chapter Two for instructions on constructing a piece mold. Divide your sculpted head into sections which are free of undercuts for easier removal of the cast. Adjustments to the model may have to be done as a compromise. Cut the clay and place shims (metal strips) to separate pieces of the mold when it is finished. Strips cut from a manilla file folder are a good substitute if metal shims are not available. Put a notch between mold parts to aid in repositioning when casting. This can be done with a Z in the shim. The head should be cast in two or three parts.

Mix plaster with bluing for the first coat of the mold to help distinguish the mold from the cast. Then continue adding plaster by sections until it is about one and one-half inch thick.

Open and remove the mold from the model and clean out the excess plasticene. Size the inside of the mold with petroleum jelly or liquid soap to aid in separation of mold and cast.

Tie the mold parts together in proper alignment and plug any holes with plasticene to prevent leaks. Mix plaster and pour in gently to prevent forming air bubbles. As plaster settles, add more plaster. When dry remove your piece and trim. Finish as desired (See Chapter Two).

Place shims or dividers in the model to divide the parts of your mold. Then add plaster, about one and one-half inches thick, to both sides of shims to form mold.

When dry, pry evenly all around the seam of the mold to loosen it from the model.

Dig out and recycle the plasticene from the open mold and prepare the mold for casting by adding a separator.

Life Casting

At one time, life casting was looked down upon because some thought of it as copying the body rather than sculpting it. This argument assumes that the artist is only a technician reproducing a body. We have only to look at the works of George Segal or Duane Hanson to see the fallacy in this statement. Artists Willa Shalit and Dean Ericson believe life casting portrays the human form in a very direct and pure way. They often use fragments and pieces to develop their expression.

Plaster is among the best and safest media for life casting, thanks largely to materials produced for industrial use but available to artists. The medical profession has long used plaster surgical gauze for making casts to help mend bone fractures. Dentists use the seaweed derivative alginate to make exact impression molds of teeth for caps and dentures. Artists can use plaster gauze for both positive and negative molds. Alginate, on the other hand, must be held together with plaster gauze while a mother mold, or outer support mold, is made.

Explosive Dancer is a life casting by Willa Shalit and Dean Ericson. The College of Santa Fe, Santa Fe, New Mexico.

Plaster Gauze Body Casting (positive)

MATERIALS

Crisco or petroleum jelly
skin moisturizing lotion
plaster gauze
finishing materials such as water-based
polyurethane, acrylic paint, Dryvit

The first step is to plan your design. Keep in mind that it isn't necessary to cast the entire body when life casting. Often, one part of the body is more expressive than the whole and automatically creates a center of interest. Visualize your selection as a sculpture meant to be seen from the inside as well as the outside. *Ritual Figures* by Dixie Friend Gay can be viewed on many levels of understanding. With careful planning, your cast can be, too.

Almost all work in plaster is best done in teams for efficiency in time as well as materials. In life casting there is also the addition of a live model whose safety is very important. Plaster gives off heat as it hardens, and the molding process includes confinement and enclosure, so the psychological effect of these factors needs to be high on the priority list. It is also important to liberally apply Crisco or petroleum jelly to any hair that may be part of the cast, or lotion to large areas of skin.

There are a number of techniques for sculpting parts of the body with plaster surgical gauze. Most of these involve casting the particular body section in two parts with an extra thick seam on the edges. The seam can be opened to release the model, after which the cast can easily be put back together.

Cast a foot by applying layers of plaster gauze to it while the model is standing. Leave a small opening at the back for easy removal. When the main portion of the foot cast is hard, cast the heel and attach it to the rest of the foot, trap door style, with plaster gauze.

Create a hard clear surface by coating the cast with acrylic medium or water-based polyurethane. Other finishing alternatives include decorative painting and troweling on a layer of Dryvit Top Coat.

(Right) Two Figures in One. **Student work by Peyton Manning. Split body cast in papier-mâché, plaster gauze mask, comic strip mâché.**

(Below) Ritual Figures, **by Dixie Friend Gay. Burlap and fiberglass. Courtesy K + B Plaza, New Orleans, Louisiana.**

Casting a Face with Alginate

MATERIALS

plaster gauze

scissors

drop cloth

shower cap

petroleum jelly or Crisco

skin moisturizing lotion

alginate

water

salt

cotton batting

plaster

hanger

X-acto knife

trowel

paint or other finish if desired

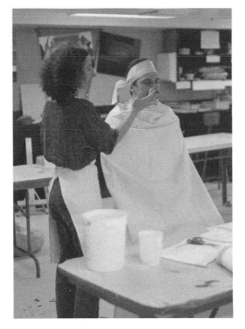

Artist Willa Shalit prepares the model by covering his clothing and hair and lubricating his facial hair.

Prepare alginate according to instructions. Gradually cover whole face with alginate, leaving the nose until last; you have four minutes until it sets.

Alginate can reproduce fine detail when used in a mold. It is safe, nontoxic and relatively easy to use. The process of casting a face with alginate is applicable to casting other parts of the body.

The first step is to prepare your materials and work area. These should be clean and well organized. Cut your plaster gauze into strips nine inches long, and arrange them in groups of three, since they will be applied in three-ply thicknesses. Stack the strips in a crisscross fashion for easy use. Cut and stack some smaller lengths for detail support.

Cover the model with a drop cloth and put a shower cap over his or her hair. Apply petroleum jelly or Crisco to the brows, lashes and any other exposed hair. Facial hair can be coated with skin moisturizing lotion. Ask the model to keep his or her eyes closed and talk to the model as you progress to alleviate any fears.

Mix one and one-eighth cups of alginate to two cups of tepid water, add some salt to quicken drying and mix vigorously

for thirty seconds. You will have approximately four minutes to apply alginate mixture before it sets to the face. Cup your hand and gradually cover the whole face, leaving the nose until last. Carefully apply alginate between the nostrils, making sure to keep the air passages open. If some of the alginate drips into the nose, have the model blow out firmly to clear. Once you notice the alginate starting to thicken, setting happens quickly.

As soon as the alginate sets, begin to adhere cotton batting by patting onto the model's face and allowing it to stick. Work from outside to inside letting it stick.

Next, apply wet plaster gauze strips to create the mother mold (support mold) for the alginate. Apply nine-inch-long strips to the face in groups of threes, covering most of the facial surface. Use the

smaller strips in threes for the eyes and mouth. Add rolls of very small pieces of gauze as extra support for nose.

Once the plaster gauze has set, remove the mold gently from the face of the model by working your fingers around the edges. Use care to keep the alginate in the mold. Close the mold's nostril holes with plaster gauze and add more support to the outside of the mold. As the plaster gauze dries and hardens, spray the alginate occasionally with water from a plant mister. It is necessary to keep the alginate moist because, if it dries, it will crumble before the plaster cast is poured.

Mix eight cups of plaster to make a one-inch layer in the mold. Slosh a thin coat of plaster called a milk coat all over the mold. When the milk coat begins to harden, pack the mold's inside contours

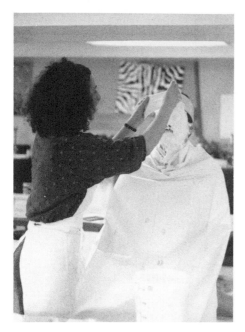

Apply loose cotton to the tacky alginate, allowing the cotton to stick. Then apply plaster gauze to the cotton and over the mask area. This becomes a mother mold to hold the alginate in place. When dry remove the mold and mist lightly to keep the alginate damp.

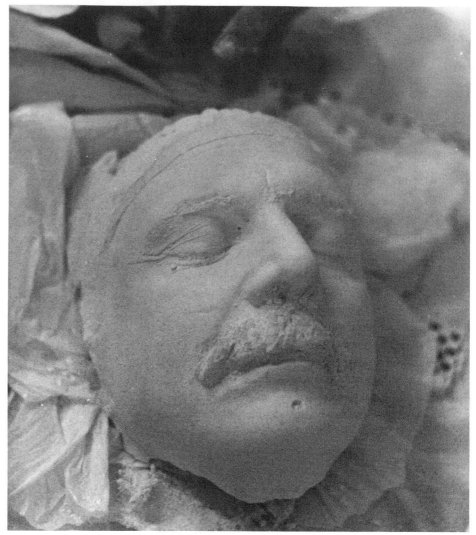

with plaster to one-inch thickness. Make a hook for hanging the cast and imbed it in back at the top.

Opening the mold is always an exciting event. Pry up the edges of the mold and peel away the layers, destroying the mold as you go. Then peel off the alginate and discover the cast. Go over the cast with an X-acto knife to remove any flaws and clean out the nostrils.

Leave the cast complete as it is, or "open" the eyes and build up the hair. First look at the model's eyes. Then draw outlines of the eyes on the closed lids of the cast. Next, carve the irises out and shape the eyeballs. Make deeper cuts for the folded lids. The eyes should align and the irises should be in the same position. The covering on the model's head casts as a shape. Determine how the hair will be arranged. Dampen the cast shape and trowel on plaster. Imitate the texture and characteristic of the model's hair.

The plaster may be left in its natural white state or finished with a painted or bronze patina (See Chapter Two).

Mix plaster and pour it into the mold. When it has set, carefully remove the cast from the mold. Seeing what's inside the mold is the most exciting part of the process.

Life cast of the author as a Roman emperor by Jayne Williams and George Wolfe. The hair was added and the eyes were carved open. A second mask uses an attached hand to create a pensive mood.

TEN

construction and assemblages

throughout history the human figure and animal forms have dominated the content of sculpture. Because of its permanence, sculpture has served to record history through images of its leaders, religious figures and common folk. Much of this artwork has been closely tied to architecture, as decoration or enhancement. While figurative work is still part of the sculpture scene, subject matter of the twentieth century has become increasingly diverse, and a variety of styles has emerged. In the early part of this century, sculpture tended to echo the dominant styles of each era. Art Nouveau, Cubism, Futurism, Surrealism and Expressionism all had outlets in three dimensions.

About the time of the Bauhaus movement in Germany, in the late 1920s and early 1930s, a new approach to design began to change sculpture. The Bauhaus school espoused the importance of interrelating the disciplines of arts and crafts.

Innovative experimental works and approaches were produced by bringing together a diversity of talent. Artists began to become interested in pure form and space. A landmark sculpture in this evolution was Constantin Brancusi's *Bird in Space*, created in 1927, which expresses the idea of a bird without actually representing one. Jean Arp experimented with organic forms for their own sake, while Alexander Calder found a way to modulate space via the invention of mobiles and stabiles. The biomorphic forms of Henry Moore return to the figure for inspiration, but with a new element, the void. Expanding industrialization and more recently the growth of high technology have turned sculpture further away from ourselves to the abstract world of ideas. Even the materials of sculpture have become so diverse that the term *mixed media* is often needed to describe them. The processes of making abstract sculptures are often not part of traditional modeling, carving, shaping, molding or casting, as shown by works known as assemblages and constructions.

An assemblage is a three-dimensional collage or free-standing work that can be considered a type of construction. It is composed of found objects either natural or human-made put together to produce a new and completely different work. The forms can be altered by sculpting or painting to reflect the sculpture's new meaning.

Louise Nevelson and Jesselyn Benson Zurik are artists who have literally taken the theme "something old, something new, something borrowed and something blue" and turned it into a personal art form. While neither artist actually worked in papier-mâché, plaster or foam, similar ideas can be assembled in these media. Casts and imprints of almost any object can be taken in plaster. Positive casts of objects or the objects themselves can be part of papier-mâché assemblages. Styrofoam's utility is endless. Besides the foam pieces themselves as works of art, they can become armatures for other media.

A construction is a sculpture made from different pieces, rather than one that is cast, modeled or carved. It can be created from raw materials but may also include found objects or just about anything that adds to the form. While most of the materials are those of the construction industry, many can be found in the junk yard.

Architectural Constructions: A Medley of Design Exercises

Jesselyn Zurick amidst her treasures, which she has made from found objects.

MATERIALS

paper
pencil
poster board
scissors
small boxes of various shapes and sizes
glue
papier-mâché
plaster or foam
finishing materials as desired

An architectural construction can have almost any form that relates to architecture. This is abstract sculpture with a purpose. It offers a wide latitude in design options while remaining practical.

The best way to understand the design process is from the experience of working through a series of design exercises. The following are introductory activities which will help students develop their understanding of architectural design. These activities are intended to stimulate ideas for the students' own constructions. They begin with planes, then progress to solids, and finally combine the two.

Begin with a series of sketches and doodles of intersecting planes and shapes to help plan your forms. First, make designs using only squares and rectangles. Then add circles and triangles to create a more complex plan.

Next try creating designs with different emphases: horizontal, vertical, circular or diagonal. To make your sketches three dimensional, choose the most interesting ones and transpose them to poster board. Cut out the shapes and fasten them together by cutting slots and joining.

The second exercise introduces design with solids. Collect numerous small boxes of different shapes and sizes. Arrange them into different configurations. When you find the configuration you like, glue the boxes together.

The third type of exercise combines planes and solids. Sticks and strings can be used to define space. A void, or empty space, can be used as a way to look through to the inside or to the other side of the construction, becoming an integral part of your overall design.

Once you have developed your concept you may want to build the construction in papier-mâché, plaster or foam. You can sometimes widen the variety by using low cost and surplus materials. Bending, cutting and scoring cardboard and poster-board can also produce creative forms. Illustration board is a good resource for building squares, triangles and other geometric shapes. Balloons are simple armatures for papier-mâché spheres and can easily be removed (by popping) when the mâché is dry. Just about anything you make in papier-mâché can also be made in plaster. Styrofoam, too, is available in a variety of forms, including sheets, packing material (such as "peanuts") and store-bought geometric shapes. Any construction you build can be finished as desired.

Design exercises from a high school architecture course.

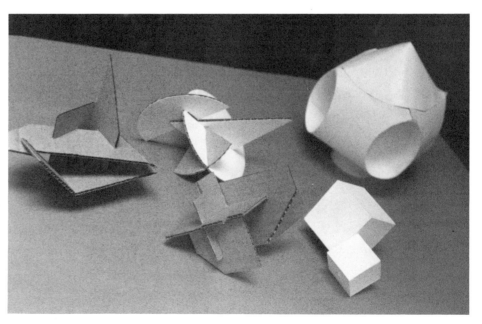

A Northwestern State University student constructed these interlocking planes and forms in cardboard. Natchitoches, Louisiana.

Free Form

The term *free form* describes work that is developed free, at least initially, of preconceived notions. Creating a free-form sculpture can be a search for form, a process of intuitive discovery in which you let your imagination work by trial and error. A free form can be a continuous shape that varies from thick to thin in convex and concave areas. Wire, screen and template armatures allow for open-ended adventures.

Wire Free Form

MATERIALS

aluminum clothesline
tape
cotton twine
burlap or cotton muslin (wire screen optional)
putty knife
rasps
wire brushes
sandpaper
finishing materials as desired

Make a simple armature of aluminum clothesline for your free form and tape the ends to a loop. Tie a couple of knots in some cotton twine, attaching it to your wire skeleton, and wrap the skeleton with the twine so it will grip plaster. String off areas that you want thicker or solid.

Pieces of burlap or muslin dipped in plaster can be laid over areas of the skeleton for your initial build up. Wire screen is another option to support shapes.

Mix a small amount of plaster and build up the form slowly with a putty knife. Continue to mix and build until your form begins to emerge. Complete your rough-in and let it dry.

Use rasps and wire brushes to shape the final form. Textures can be added, left rough or sanded smooth as the last step before adding the finish (See Chapter Two, *Finishes*).

Wire Screen Free Form

MATERIALS

wire window screen
plaster
water
finishing materials as desired.

Fashion a small piece of sculpture by bending, creasing and stretching wire window screen to create a free-form shape. The screen form will serve as the armature for your sculpture.

Mix plaster slightly thin, and dip your armature into it or ladle the wet plaster onto the screen to build up your form. Build your form by troweling on more plaster as each layer hardens or layer in some plaster-soaked cloth as you build for added strength. The screen is only the armature; let your shape grow and develop as you go.

Allow the sculpture to dry. Add final shaping, texture and decoration as desired.

WIRE FREE FORM

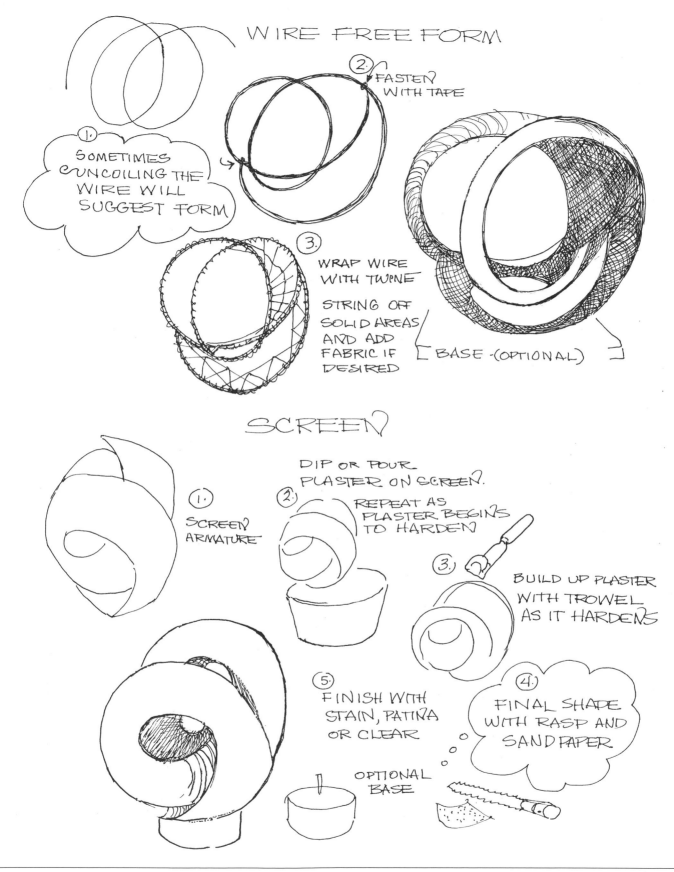

1. SOMETIMES UNCOILING THE WIRE WILL SUGGEST FORM

2. FASTEN WITH TAPE

3. WRAP WIRE WITH TWINE

STRING OFF SOLID AREAS AND ADD FABRIC IF DESIRED

BASE (OPTIONAL)

SCREEN

1. SCREEN ARMATURE

2. DIP OR POUR PLASTER ON SCREEN. REPEAT AS PLASTER BEGINS TO HARDEN

3. BUILD UP PLASTER WITH TROWEL AS IT HARDENS

4. FINAL SHADE WITH RASP AND SANDPAPER

5. FINISH WITH STAIN, PATINA OR CLEAR

OPTIONAL BASE

Carved Forms

While free form is an *additive* process, whereby the artist builds up sculptural forms on an armature, the term *carved form* implies the *subtractive* process of cutting and shaping to create forms.

Plaster and Styrofoam are commonly used in the classroom as carving material, although plaster must be prepared first. Start by collecting paper milk cartons, ice cream boxes and any other waxed or lined containers to use as molds to form plaster blocks and slabs. When you mix your plaster, try adding some cat litter as a filler for easier carving. Lay out your design on the block and rough in your form (follow steps in Chapter Two under *Carving*).

For a more unusual plaster sculpture, try adding ice cubes to the mix. Pierce a hole in the bottom of the carton or container to allow the melting ice to drain. When dry, you will have a plaster block with random spaces like swiss cheese. Cut and shape your form intuitively using the accidental irregularities produced by the ice to create a free-design piece.

Styrofoam Sculpture

MATERIALS

Styrofoam (block, salvaged packing material or sheets)
Elmer's SAF-T Contact Cement
low-voltage hot wire
surform planer or wood rasp
large plastic bag
Finish options: materials for papier-mâché or plaster, fiberglass tape, plaster or joint cement

One of the advantages of Styrofoam is that while you're carving you can build up shapes in other parts of the sculpture by gluing on pieces in any direction with Elmer's SAF-T Contact Cement or comparable adhesive. Begin with a block of Styrofoam, a collection of salvaged packing shapes or a number of sheets laminated with adhesive to form your shape.

Rough in your big shapes with a low-voltage hot wire, then switch to a Stanley Surform planer or wood rasp. Be careful to contain the little beads of Styrofoam residue, as they can take over your rooms, sink traps and lawns. Put the piece inside a large plastic bag when filing and try to contain the excess as much as possible while working.

•SAFETY NOTE: This activity is suitable only for adults or students of at least high school age. Individuals using electrical equipment in the classroom must be properly trained and closely supervised. Make sure all power and electrical tools are turned off when not in use.

When your shape is refined and you are ready for the finished surface there are a number of options. You may cover it with papier-mâché or layers of plaster and finish. Another alternative is to cover your form's surface with fiberglass tape (used for plasterboard) to strengthen your form before building it up with plaster or joint cement. Add white glue to your plaster mix for stronger finish coats.

Sculptor Rivers Murphy assembling his construction.

Styrofoam packing parts open a whole new world of assemblages and constructions. Here, a sculpture is ready for finishing.

The Template as Sculpture

MATERIALS

corrugated paper

scissors

Elmer's SAF-T Contact Cement or 3M #30 NF Contact Cement

brush

kraft paper

A simple cardboard template as a silhouette of your form is all you need to build a papier-mâché piece when using Elmer's SAF-T Contact Cement or 3M #30 NF Contact Cement.

• **SAFETY NOTE:** Use 3M #30 NF Contact Cement in a well-ventilated area. Elmer's SAF-T Contact Cement is a non-toxic alternative.

Cut corrugated paper into strips and coat with adhesive using a brush. Also coat the edges of the template. Let dry for half an hour or until dry. Now build any curved, straight or bent forms by pressing the sticking pieces of the material to the template and to each other. Overlay and join pieces to form continuous shapes. The center of your piece should be hollow except for the template. Your whole form will actually be built of these strips with the template only used as a guide (See Chapter One, *The Contact Method*).

Follow the corrugated paper with layers of kraft paper. Keep the pieces small and overlapping layer by layer, producing a smooth, continuous surface.

The original template drawn for this sculpture was converted from 2-D to 3-D by building up mâchéd pieces of corrugated paper. Sculptor Julian Strock.

Modular Structures

MATERIALS

Objects for molds and casts
such as paper and Styrofoam cups
saucers
egg cartons
fruit and vegetable liners
plastic Easter eggs and other module-like
    household objects
papier-mâché
plaster
plastic straws or dowels
plaster gauze

The influence of modular architecture is present in our lives even without our realizing it. Institutional chairs come in lock sets for easy transport and storage. Interior office modules and the sculptural quality of the window treatments on many new buildings are further examples of this influence. Architect Moshe Safdie's exhibit at Expo 67 (Montreal) called "Habitat" demonstrated how modules can be stacked and arranged to create a dynamic living space.

Found objects from everyday life are the best resources for experimenting with modules in the art classroom. Products such as paper or Styrofoam cups, egg cartons and fruit and vegetable liners can be cut and arranged as modules for papier-mâché pieces. These can also be used as molds for plaster castings to be arranged and rearranged, just as modular parts of building interiors or playground equipment are moved about. Some of these objects can be the sources of carved models, which can themselves be molded and cast as new modules.

Styrofoam packing pieces come in an infinite variety of shapes which need only be arranged and glued together to become sculpture. Cutting apart segments and arranging them in modular configurations produces a whole world of possibilities.

Once you have identified your pieces and how they are going to be used, you can fashion connections. When casting in plaster it is important to place a straw in the paper cup, egg carton or other found object to retain a hole for ease of assembling with other objects. Connections can also be made with straws or dowels glued together in place.

Found objects are often the best resource for developing modules. Paper parts can be built right into the mâché. Cups, egg cartons and plastic Easter eggs make creative molds. You can also make your own molds out of clay.

Diagram of Moshe Safdie's "Habitat."

Draped Sculpture

MATERIALS

Dress mannequin or chicken wire armature
urethane foam
papier-mâché
plaster gauze
Dip 'N' Drape
plaster-soaked fabric or clothe-mâché
white glue
water
finishing materials as desired

Draped sculpture is a long-overlooked art form which presents a novel way to conceive of a work—by its skin. While papier-mâché and plaster are the media recommended in this lesson, foam can also be used. Illustrated work by Muriel Castanis is an example of draped sculpture, where the drape of a sculpture becomes a form that can stand by itself without armature.

Old dress mannequins have become available as small town department stores and shops have given way to the Wal-Marts of our world. One mannequin can be used repeatedly as a temporary armature (model) for drape sculpture. The body shape can be changed easily by layering urethane foam as padding. And, because of its moveable parts, the mannequin can pose however the artist desires.

The artist who in not able to acquire a mannequin can design and build an armature of chicken wire as an alternative (See Chapter Nine, *Chicken Wire Figure*). Preliminary sketches may help the artist generate ideas for creative armatures.

Today's readily available materials, including papier-mâché, make draping easy. Plaster surgical gauze dries rapidly and if applied thickly enough can stand as a shell. Dip 'N' Drape is an excellent product, but it does require a permanent arma-ture, as does plaster-soaked fabric. White glue and water sprayed on clothing or drapery in layers produces a hard surface known as clothe-mâché. This medium also requires a permanent armature. Any of these sculptures can be finished and painted as desired.

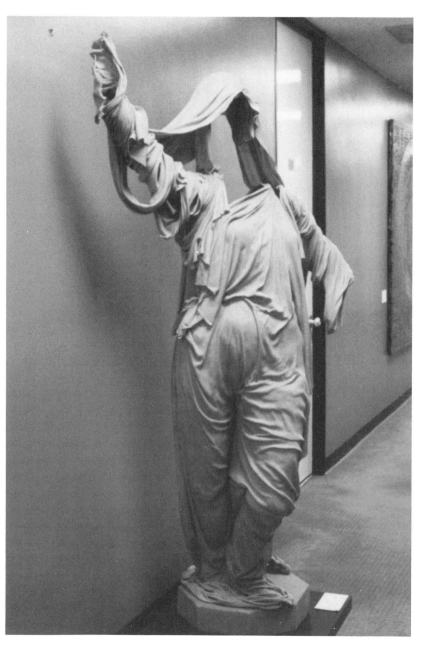

Muriel Castanis' *Patina VI* is a draped sculpture of a robe without its wearer! Courtesy of the Virlane Foundation, New Orleans, Louisiana.

Larger-than-life assemblages and constructions found in living and working spaces are known as environment or environmental art. As an extension of collage, environmental art shares space with its viewers and is frequently intended to be moved among or through, rather than merely viewed. The elements used to build environmental assemblages and constructions are most often found objects or painted and sculpted pieces. Papier-mâché, plaster and foam, or any combination of them, are all workable materials for environmental art. When they are finished with weather-resistant materials they may even be placed outdoors.

Large Outdoor Sculpture

MATERIALS

Styrofoam (blocks, packing pieces or sheets laminated with Elmer's SAF-T Contact Cement)
saws and Styrofoam cutter
Surform planer or wood rasp
sandpaper
Primus Adhesive
white portland cement
fiberglass mesh
Dryvit Top Coat
trowel

With the arrival of new surfacing materials to protect it from the elements, Styrofoam has found a new life in large outdoor sculpture. Artists can use either packing pieces, a block or sheets laminated together with Elmer's SAF-T Contact Cement. Packing pieces can be especially interesting to work with because they provide ready-made forms.

The biggest challenge will be designing a base. While most sculpture needs something to hold it up, Styrofoam needs something to hold it down. It's important for the artist to consider the base early in the planning and design stage, because it may be necessary for it to become part of the sculpture itself.

Once the form is assembled and carved to your liking, it's ready to finish. For a hard concrete finish suitable for outdoors, use Dryvit. This is a product used in the construction of many buildings today. It is readily available, fun to use and extremely durable. For maximum strength, coat your Styrofoam form with a fifty-fifty mix of Primus Adhesive and portland cement (white), then a layer of fiberglass mesh. After this is dry, trowel a sixteenth-inch layer of Dryvit Top Coat over the whole surface. When dry this coating will produce an extremely hard cementicious acrylic surface (See Chapter Three, *Styrofoam and the Dryvit System*).

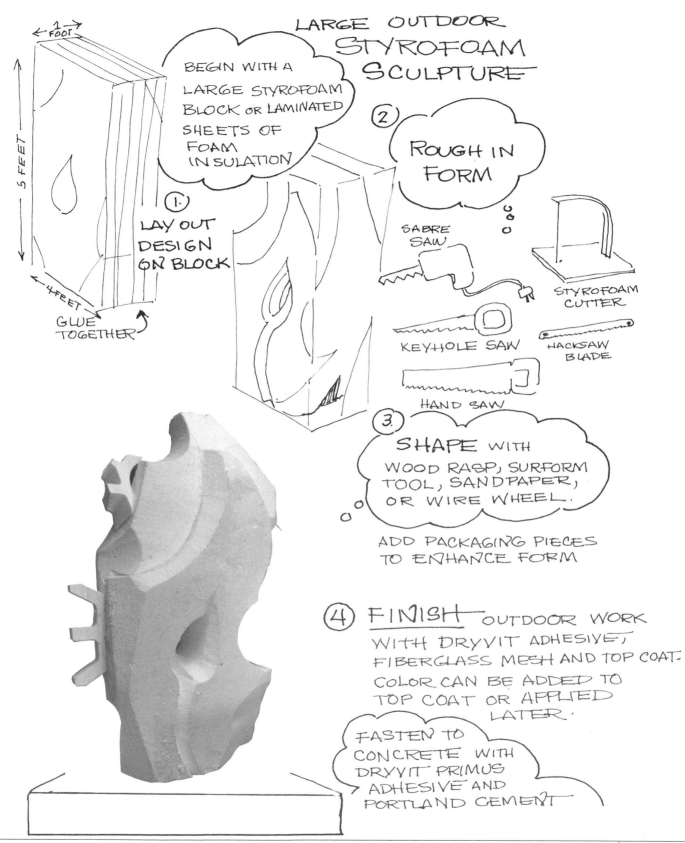

LARGE OUTDOOR
STYROFOAM
SCULPTURE

1 FOOT

5 FEET

4 FEET

GLUE TOGETHER

① LAY OUT DESIGN ON BLOCK

BEGIN WITH A LARGE STYROFOAM BLOCK OR LAMINATED SHEETS OF FOAM INSULATION

② ROUGH IN FORM

SABRE SAW

STYROFOAM CUTTER

KEYHOLE SAW

HACKSAW BLADE

HAND SAW

③ SHAPE WITH WOOD RASP, SURFORM TOOL, SANDPAPER, OR WIRE WHEEL.

ADD PACKAGING PIECES TO ENHANCE FORM

④ FINISH OUTDOOR WORK WITH DRYVIT ADHESIVE, FIBERGLASS MESH AND TOP COAT. COLOR CAN BE ADDED TO TOP COAT OR APPLIED LATER.

FASTEN TO CONCRETE WITH DRYVIT PRIMUS ADHESIVE AND PORTLAND CEMENT

THE 4 FOUR STORY DRAGON

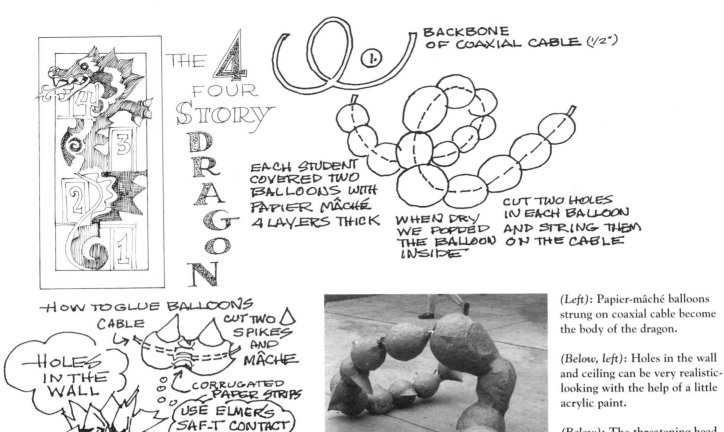

BACKBONE OF COAXIAL CABLE (1/2")

①.

EACH STUDENT COVERED TWO BALLOONS WITH PAPIER MÂCHÉ 4 LAYERS THICK

WHEN DRY WE POPPED THE BALLOON INSIDE

CUT TWO HOLES IN EACH BALLOON AND STRING THEM ON THE CABLE

HOW TO GLUE BALLOONS

CABLE

CUT TWO SPIKES AND MÂCHÉ

CORRUGATED PAPER STRIPS

USE ELMER'S SAF-T CONTACT CEMENT

HOLES IN THE WALL

CUT AND SCORED CARDBOARD

PAINT INSIDE BLACK

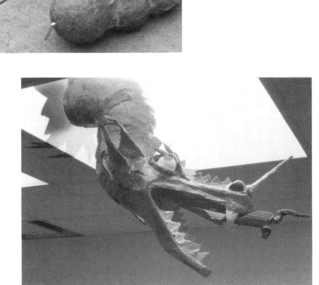

(Left): Papier-mâché balloons strung on coaxial cable become the body of the dragon.

(Below, left): Holes in the wall and ceiling can be very realistic-looking with the help of a little acrylic paint.

(Below): The threatening head of the dragon emerging from the skylight is enough to frighten any would-be science student!

The Four Story Dragon

MATERIALS

coaxial cable scraps
balloons
strip papier-mâché
corrugated paper
Styrofoam
scored cardboard
Elmer's SAF-T Contact Cement
acrylic paints
wire
nails

The art club at the Isidore Newman School in New Orleans built this dragon as part of an effort made by the school to decorate certain areas including the stairwell. Using clever imagination, the students designed a dragon that appears to burst through the stairwell walls, threading its way up to the fourth floor. Its head breaks through the ceiling just outside of the science lab.

The concept itself is a simple one. The segmented body is made from a "spine" of coaxial cable (scraps are available from cable TV companies) threaded through papier-mâché spheres made from balloons. The "holes" in the wall are made of jagged pieces of Styrofoam and cut and scored cardboard. Finally, its head is made of contact mâché.

The dragon itself is suspended from the ceiling and wall with wire, and from the stairs with a C-clamp. The "holes" are nailed to the walls.

ELEVEN

all the world's a stage

Works in Progress

A how-to book is great to generate ideas, but somewhere along the way we need to see how these ideas can be put in context. I've had teachers tell me they have had trouble getting their students to do something different and challenging. Sometimes all the students need is a little push to build momentum. Unlike students of the performing arts, studio art students often work alone on their own ideas and creations. While the artroom atmosphere can help students generate ideas based on their own observations, their motivation may increase when they work together as a team. Group dynamics breed fresh ideas. If you work on projects that fill a need, you can open doors that your students didn't know were there. You can easily create motivation by taking advantage of some of those unwanted projects, like homecoming decorations, scenery and costumes for plays, or parade props, and turn them into your own projects. You and your students may be surprised at what the combination of group dynamics and imagination can produce!

Alice, a play based on Lewis Carroll's *Alice in Wonderland*, was one of those opportunities. A team of student designers created costumes for a story they knew as children, which augmented the idea of simply making costumes. The play needed a host of creatures—the White Rabbit, a Griffin, the Mad Hatter, the Mock Turtle, the Dormouse, Frog Footman and Fish Footman, to name a few. Urethane foam was the answer. Many of the techniques used for headpieces (Chapter Six) could be used for costumes for *Alice*.

The White Rabbit costume is simply ears of foam on a headband and a cotton tail worn with whatever fanciful clothing you can find. The Griffin costume is a combination of a headpiece, based on the bird headpiece, and a poncho-like cape. The Mock Turtle's shell is made from a large piece of poster board. Cut and overlap the board to make a three-dimensional shell, then glue it to a vest made of foam. The Turtle's head can be made out of foam or you can paint the actor's face instead.

A sleeveless tuxedo cape becomes a base costume for the Mad Hatter, the Frog Footman and the Fish Footman. Make the Mad Hatter's stovepipe hat out of foam lined with poster board for support. An extra ring of piping should be added to the inside edge of the hat for strength. Score the bottom side of the tuxedo tails and add wire if you want the tails to stick out. Glue the Frog Footman's hind legs to the sides of the tuxedo or replace the tuxedo tails with the Fish Footman's tail. Use the techniques for the origami method headpiece for the two Footmen, starting with a diamond of foam. Even the Dormouse headpiece and two-way headpiece—a baby bonnet that reverses into a pig—can be made of foam.

Alice turned out be a wonderful opportunity in disguise.
Isidore Newman School, New Orleans, Louisiana.
Costume design by the author.

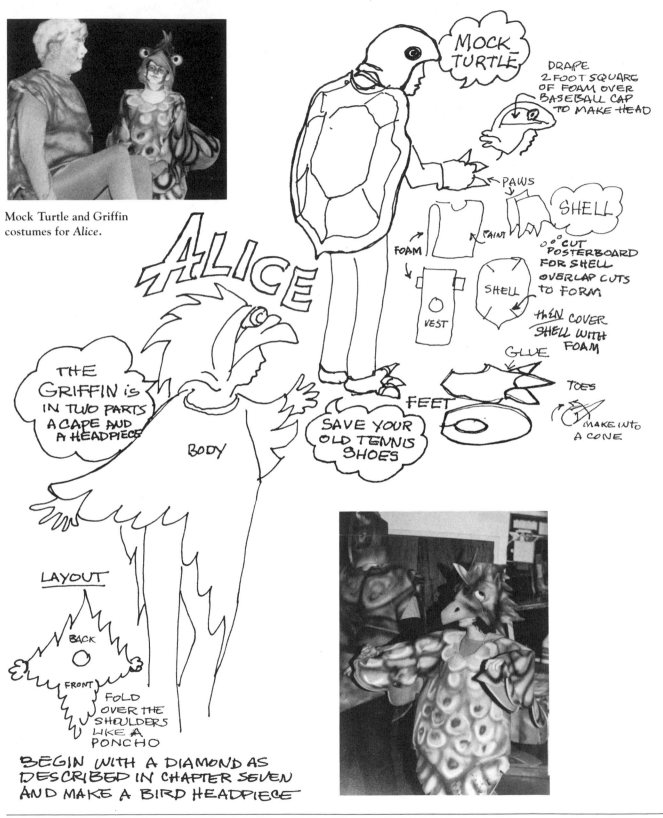

Mock Turtle and Griffin costumes for *Alice*.

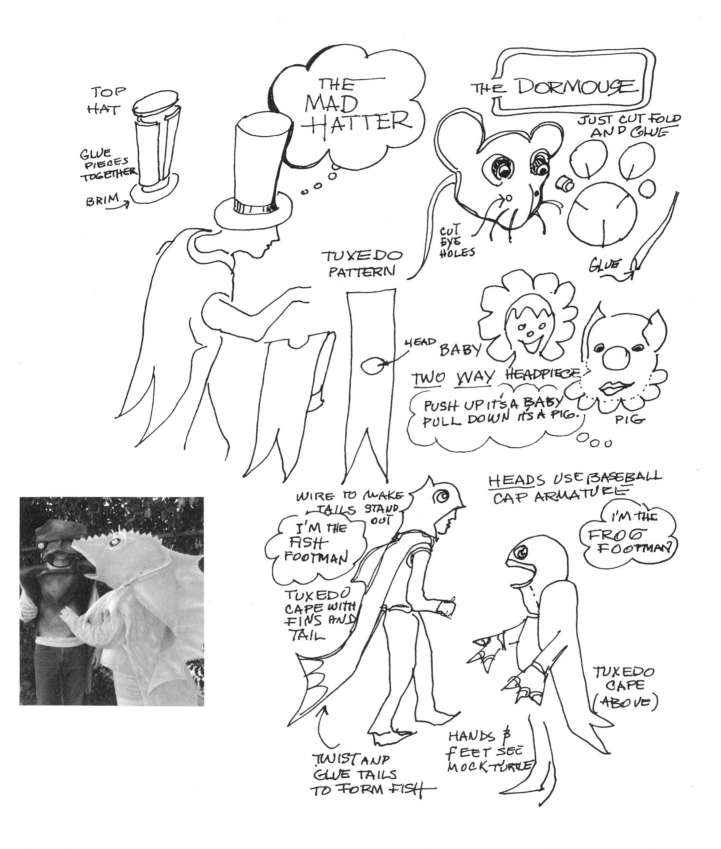

GLUE EDGES

NO GLUE HERE

NOSE

PIPING
CUT A STRIP OF FOAM, FOLD AND GLUE. USE THIS FOR OUTLINING DETAILS.

WILD THINGS

ORIGAMI FOLD CREATURE

START WITH A DIAMOND

FOLD

ORIGAMI FOLDS

INSET EYES IN FOLD

TONGUE GLUE TWO FOAM STRIPS TOGETHER WITH WIRE BETWEEN

WIRE

EARS

BROW

TIE A KNOT

NOSE

KNOT

HEAD

Where the Wild Things Are, an adaptation of a children's book by Maurice Sendak, creates a forum for urethane foam headpieces, masks and body puppets. Such a play could easily be modified for actors of different ages as a video production. Video allows you to exaggerate scale and create moods not easily done on the stage.

Sandwich masks (Chapter Five) and the origami headpiece (Chapter Six) work well for larger scale presentations. You can also fashion a long-haired, long-nosed headpiece using a baseball cap as an armature. Extend the bill with cardboard. Then add a strip of foam folded in lots of ridges to the top of the bill for the nose. Jagged teeth go underneath the bill. Lots of hair and large paint can lid eyes are particularly dramatic. Cut a long tunic of foam with a hole for the head. Tuck and glue the tunic around the body of the wearer.

A larger-than-life creature is a backpack frame and plastic pipes disguised in foam.

A slit cut partway up the front and back can be tucked between the wearer's legs and glued to make pants. Tie a naval in front and spray paint a circle pattern around it to further exaggerate the body.

You also might consider the larger-than-life puppets in Chapter Eight. One can be made easily with the help of an old backpack frame. To extend the frame, slide PVC pipe into the vertical bars, drill holes and pin in place. Then add a double loop of three-quarter inch polyethylene pipe to each extension. Cover the pipes with cylinders of foam. Lightly wrap and tie the cylinders with string before adding foam ribbing. Foam balls inside scored poster board ovals covered with foam make interesting, even eery, eyes. Add teeth, spikes and other details as desired.

For an artist *Little Shop of Horrors* offers the chance of a lifetime. You can do a stage design that will carry the show. Creative opportunities abound in the four stages of Audrey II—a plant that takes over the stage and grows up to eat people.

Audrey II #1 starts out as a handpuppet emerging from a plant pot. The pot itself sits on a table. The table top has a hole in it, through which a puppeteer stationed underneath manipulates the handpuppet. In the second stage, the puppeteer actor holds the pot and operates a larger Audrey II handpuppet. A stuffed arm attached to the outside of the pot becomes the actor's arm. From the third stage on Audrey II is essentially a body puppet. It moves and sings, elongating its neck as it grows.

Audrey II #1 is a hand puppet emerging from a plant pot.

Creatures utilizing sandwich masks of urethane foam were a natural for wild things. Cut-and-fold foam masks are good options, too.

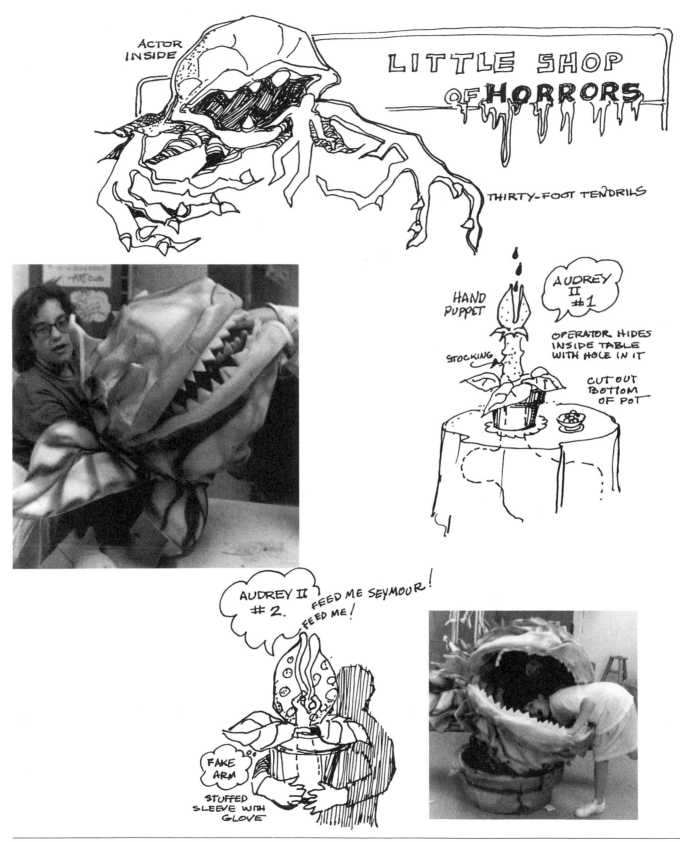

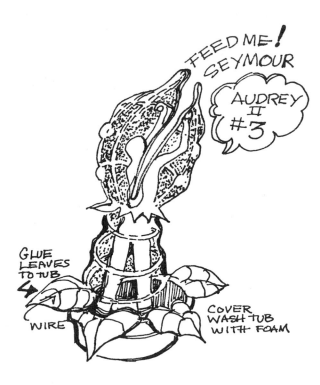

FEED ME! SEYMOUR

AUDREY II #3

GLUE LEAVES TO TUB

WIRE

COVER WASH TUB WITH FOAM

STUDENT DANIEL KERN MAKING THE ARMATURE COME ALIVE

The armature for the final stage of Audrey is over six feet in diameter and is made of plastic pipe on a backpack frame. Its thirty-foot tendrils and hinged arms are made of light plastic electrical conduit with coaxial cable scraps for fingers. If coaxial cable is not available, try heating and bending pieces of conduit. Cover the entire armature with urethane foam.

Stage people in green scrub suits and Audrey headpieces manipulate the huge tendrils to feed the plant. More people with hand puppets continue the illusion of an omnivorous plant.

Audrey, designed by the author and made by Isidore Newman School students.

Spanish language students created papier-mâché and plaster masks for *Los Fantoches*, a Mexican folk play about the burning of Judas which they dramatized as a video production. Video is a great way for untrained actors to get around the fear of an audience. A little video editing helps make this sort of project possible with limited time and materials.

The play itself features lifesize or larger puppets (los fantoches) made of papier-mâché. The puppets eventually meet "Fate" (a character) and are blown up one at a time in a fireworks display. Cut-and-fold masks, with scored paper features, and plaster gauze masks are easiest to make for such productions (See Chapter Five).

Stage and Festival Regalia

For many people, the idea of Camelot is a real part of life. The knight in shining armor still has a place in our world, if only for an escape or, in this case, a festival. Medieval and Renaissance festivals are annual events in many towns. They are for children, but they do allow adults an opportunity to become kids again, if only for a little while. Probably the most valid reason for making armor and weapons is for theater props. Regalia of this nature also works well in parades.

These props are especially useful for school productions because they are inexpensive and easy to make. Surplus material can often be found to reduce cost.

(Above) Student Lindsey York transforms a plaster gauze lift of her own face into a skull for the play.

(Left) Actors show the masks they will wear in the traditional Mexican folk play, "Los Fantoches." Courtesy Jeff Cole.

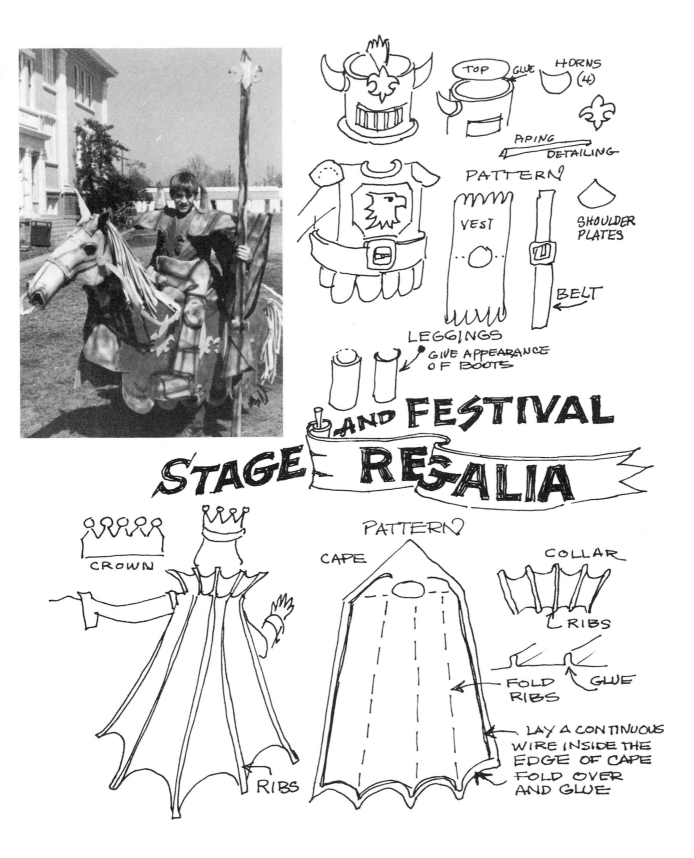

HORNS (4)

TOP GLUE

PIPING
DETAILING

PATTERN

VEST

SHOULDER PLATES

BELT

LEGGINGS
GIVE APPEARANCE OF BOOTS

STAGE AND FESTIVAL REGALIA

CROWN

CAPE

PATTERN

COLLAR

RIBS

FOLD RIBS

GLUE

LAY A CONTINUOUS WIRE INSIDE THE EDGE OF CAPE FOLD OVER AND GLUE

RIBS

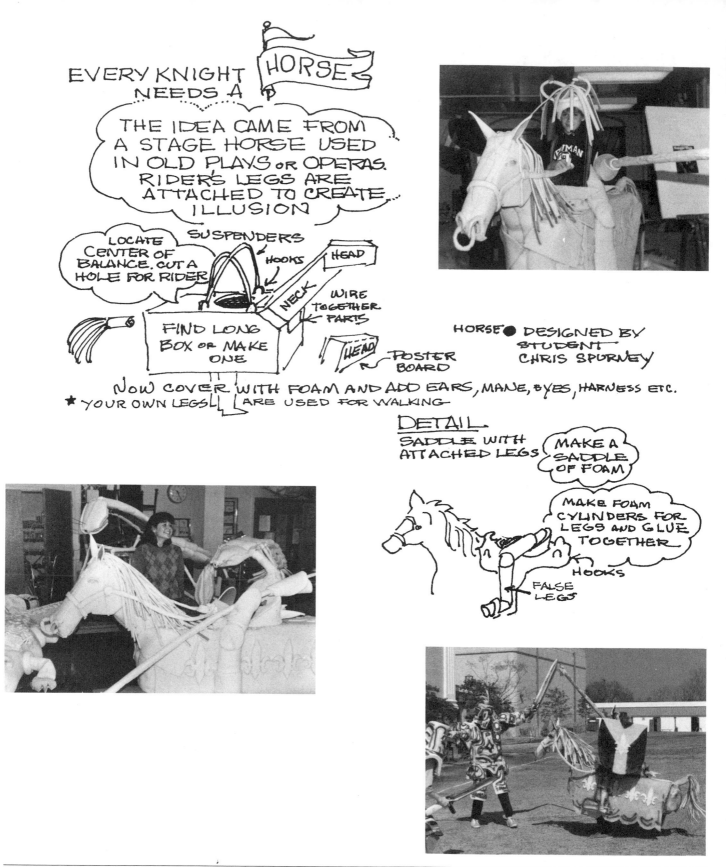

EVERY KNIGHT NEEDS A **HORSE**

THE IDEA CAME FROM A STAGE HORSE USED IN OLD PLAYS or OPERAS. RIDER'S LEGS ARE ATTACHED TO CREATE ILLUSION

LOCATE CENTER OF BALANCE. CUT A HOLE FOR RIDER

SUSPENDERS

HOOKS

HEAD

NECK

WIRE TOGETHER PARTS

FIND LONG BOX OR MAKE ONE

HEAD

POSTER BOARD

HORSE● DESIGNED BY STUDENT CHRIS SPURNEY

NOW COVER WITH FOAM AND ADD EARS, MANE, EYES, HARNESS ETC.

★ YOUR OWN LEGS ARE USED FOR WALKING

DETAIL
SADDLE WITH ATTACHED LEGS

MAKE A SADDLE OF FOAM

MAKE FOAM CYLINDERS FOR LEGS AND GLUE TOGETHER

HOOKS

FALSE LEGS

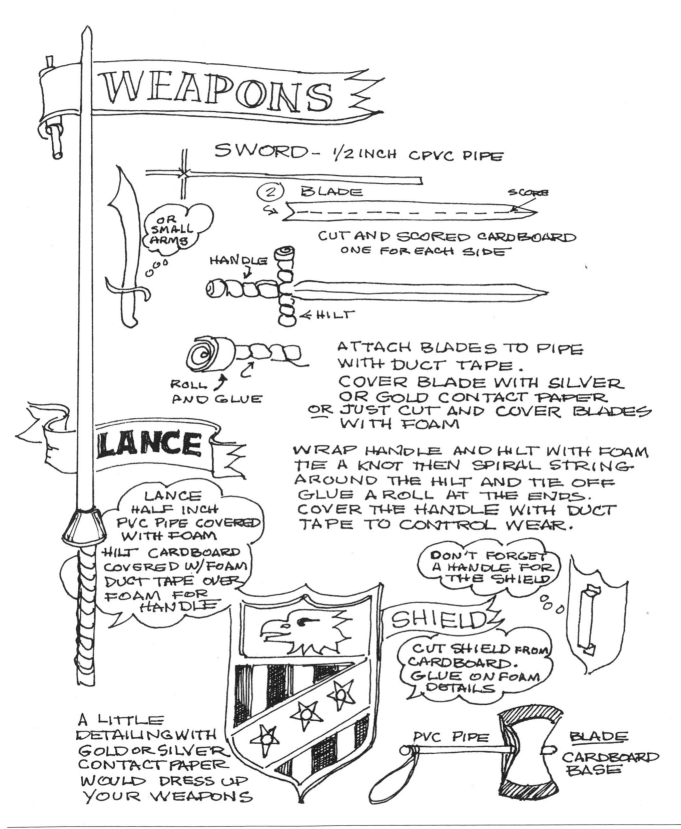

WEAPONS

SWORD- 1/2 INCH CPVC PIPE

(2) BLADE   SCORE

CUT AND SCORED CARDBOARD
ONE FOR EACH SIDE

OR SMALL ARMS

HANDLE

HILT

ROLL AND GLUE

ATTACH BLADES TO PIPE
WITH DUCT TAPE.
COVER BLADE WITH SILVER
OR GOLD CONTACT PAPER
OR JUST CUT AND COVER BLADES
WITH FOAM

WRAP HANDLE AND HILT WITH FOAM
TIE A KNOT THEN SPIRAL STRING
AROUND THE HILT AND TIE OFF
GLUE A ROLL AT THE ENDS.
COVER THE HANDLE WITH DUCT
TAPE TO CONTROL WEAR.

LANCE

LANCE
HALF INCH
PVC PIPE COVERED
WITH FOAM
HILT CARDBOARD
COVERED W/ FOAM
DUCT TAPE OVER
FOAM FOR
HANDLE

DON'T FORGET
A HANDLE FOR
THE SHIELD

SHIELD

CUT SHIELD FROM
CARDBOARD.
GLUE ON FOAM
DETAILS

A LITTLE
DETAILING WITH
GOLD OR SILVER
CONTACT PAPER
WOULD DRESS UP
YOUR WEAPONS

PVC PIPE

BLADE
CARDBOARD
BASE

On Display

Papier-mâché, plaster and foam go beyond the stage and festival, and make quite a splash in the display arena. These materials, along with some imagination and creativity, will beat signs and posters hands down at announcing events like exhibits, benefits, school dances and other functions. The uniqueness of such a display, or a combination of a display and posters, may even be enough to increase the function's attendance over that drawn by posters alone. The display can then be moved to the entrance of the function site where it will serve to welcome the attendees as they arrive.

The Victorian hot air balloon was a window display for the Historic New Orleans Collection exhibit, *A Pelican's Eye View*. To make a similar work, begin with a large balloon and cover it with foil. Apply papier-mâché layers. Covering the papier-mâché balloon with urethane foam hides imperfections and accepts paint

well. Attach a wicker basket and added frills, bows and beads to simulate a Victorian hot air balloon.

Bananas can take on human characteristics with some imagination and urethane foam. "Bananas Dance" was a stage centerpiece for a gala fundraiser and dance called "Carnival in Rio." This banana couple dances à la Carmen Miranda.

Cut a template of foam core. Tape a four-foot piece of half-inch PVC pipe to the template. Make a stand of three-eighths-inch zinc pipe. Add urethane foam scraps for stuffing, covering the banana one side at a time by gluing them to the template.

Use a real banana as a model and cut four peelings from urethane foam. Add light wire to the edges. Bring up all peelings to cover the banana, then roll back some for that peeled effect. Add features to help animate the banana and create a center of attention.

VICTORIAN HOT AIR BALLOON

CONSTRUCTION DETAILS

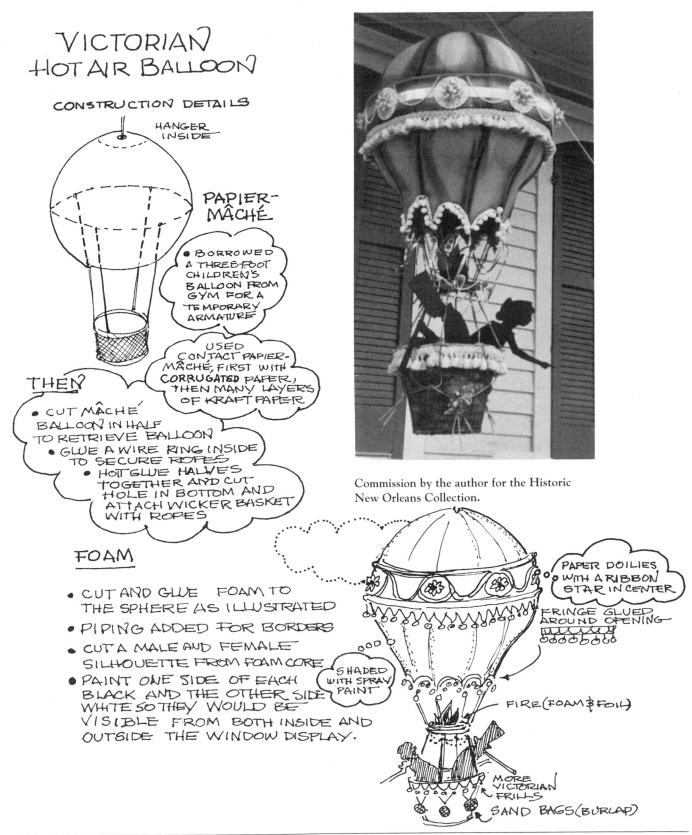

HANGER INSIDE

PAPIER-MÂCHÉ

- BORROWED A THREE-FOOT CHILDREN'S BALLOON FROM GYM FOR A TEMPORARY ARMATURE
- USED CONTACT PAPIER-MÂCHÉ, FIRST WITH CORRUGATED PAPER, THEN MANY LAYERS OF KRAFT PAPER

THEN

- CUT MÂCHÉ BALLOON IN HALF TO RETRIEVE BALLOON
- GLUE A WIRE RING INSIDE TO SECURE ROPES
- HOT GLUE HALVES TOGETHER AND CUT HOLE IN BOTTOM AND ATTACH WICKER BASKET WITH ROPES

Commission by the author for the Historic New Orleans Collection.

FOAM

- CUT AND GLUE FOAM TO THE SPHERE AS ILLUSTRATED
- PIPING ADDED FOR BORDERS
- CUT A MALE AND FEMALE SILHOUETTE FROM FOAM CORE
- PAINT ONE SIDE OF EACH BLACK AND THE OTHER SIDE WHITE SO THEY WOULD BE VISIBLE FROM BOTH INSIDE AND OUTSIDE THE WINDOW DISPLAY.

PAPER DOILIES WITH A RIBBON STAR IN CENTER

FRINGE GLUED AROUND OPENING

SHADED WITH SPRAY PAINT

FIRE (FOAM & FOIL)

MORE VICTORIAN FRILLS

SAND BAGS (BURLAP)

Many of the sculptural forms and techniques discussed in this book can be used on parade. Masks, headpieces, body puppets and creatures real or imaginary can all become parts of the larger-than-life works created primarily for parades.

The mini float, *The Bad Seed,* was produced for Mardi Gras as part of a grant from the National Endowment for the Arts through the Contemporary Art Center, New Orleans, by Isidore Newman High School students.

It began as a multidisciplinary project combining theater, art and music inspired by the play *The Bad Seed,* based on the novel of the same name by William March. The result was a dragon breathing fire and a volcano oozing green slime, both of which were riding on a pink cloud. Helium-filled balloons in the school colors left over from homecoming were released from the volcano while a huge tongue darted from the dragon's mouth. A simple system of a ramp, rollerskates and a rope animated the head. The float was actually an interpretation of the play's title, as opposed to its theme, but the class paid homage to the play by planting large seed packets on the float.

The dragon was made from cardboard boxes and end cuts for spikes. The volcano was made of chicken wire and papier-mâché. Old bed sheets stretched over plywood templates formed the clouds on the sides. To complete the ensemble, students made dragon headpieces (Chapter Six) and silkscreened their logo on inside-out gym T-shirts.

MINI-FLOAT
SKETCH

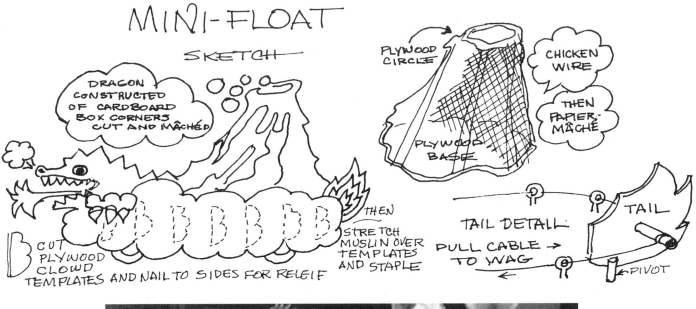

DRAGON CONSTRUCTED OF CARDBOARD BOX CORNERS CUT AND MÂCHÉD

PLYWOOD CIRCLE

CHICKEN WIRE

THEN PAPIER-MÂCHÉ

PLYWOOD BASE

CUT PLYWOOD CLOWD TEMPLATES AND NAIL TO SIDES FOR RELEIF

THEN STRETCH MUSLIN OVER TEMPLATES AND STAPLE

TAIL DETAIL

PULL CABLE TO WAG

TAIL

PIVOT

TONGUE MECHANISM DETAIL

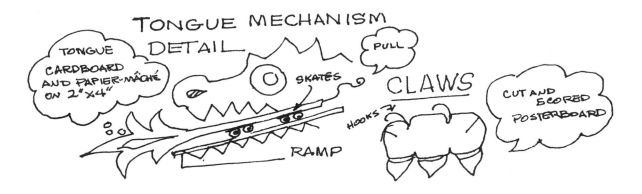

TONGUE CARDBOARD AND PAPIER-MÂCHÉ ON 2"x4"

PULL

SKATES

RAMP

CLAWS

HOOKS

CUT AND SCORED POSTERBOARD

The Crawfish is a scavenger that will survive any way it can. Here we illustrate two ways to create the same creature.

Student Lee Lovejoy plans to march his crawfish in a parade and will be seen from within a crowd of fellow marchers. For this reason his crawfish had to be constructed using an extended homemade backpack frame and plastic pipe as an armature. Its foam head and claws, which will rise high above the marchers' heads, will now be visible to spectators.

Joan André, art teacher from Clearwood Middle School in Slidell, Louisiana, designed her crawfish as a party costume for the opening night of a convention. Had she chosen a design like Lee Lovejoy's, she probably wouldn't have been able to participate in the Cajun Two-Step!

Marching crawfish by student Lee Lovejoy.

The armature for the urethane foam marching crawfish is made of plastic pipe and cardboard added to a homemade backpack frame.

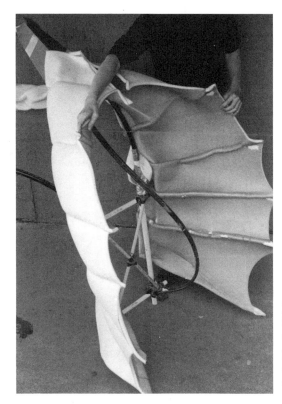

Make the back out of urethane foam by ribbing and gluing inside-out. Glue the points together first. Add a ribbed piece of foam at the bottom for a tail. A continuous wire around the outside edge of the tail will help it stand out.

Getting to Work

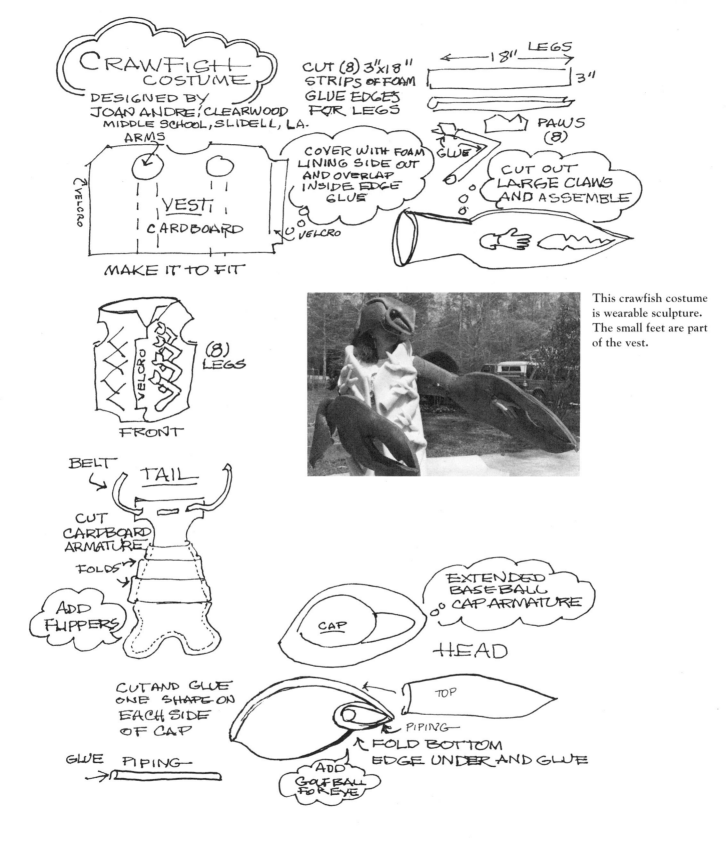

CRAWFISH COSTUME

DESIGNED BY JOAN ANDRE, CLEARWOOD MIDDLE SCHOOL, SLIDELL, LA.

CUT (8) 3"×18" STRIPS OF FOAM GLUE EDGES FOR LEGS

18" LEGS
3"

PAWS (8)
GLUE

ARMS
VELCRO
VEST
CARDBOARD
MAKE IT TO FIT
VELCRO

COVER WITH FOAM LINING SIDE OUT AND OVERLAP INSIDE EDGE GLUE

CUT OUT LARGE CLAWS AND ASSEMBLE

VELCRO
(8) LEGS
FRONT

This crawfish costume is wearable sculpture. The small feet are part of the vest.

BELT
TAIL
CUT CARDBOARD ARMATURE
FOLDS
ADD FLIPPERS

EXTENDED BASEBALL CAP ARMATURE
CAP
HEAD

CUT AND GLUE ONE SHAPE ON EACH SIDE OF CAP

GLUE PIPING

TOP
PIPING
FOLD BOTTOM EDGE UNDER AND GLUE
ADD GOLFBALL FOR EYE

The parade is the thing for the art club at Isidore Newman School.

Dragons of New Orleans. Carnival Marching Club founded by the author. Photograph: Jonathan Postal.

What would a parade be without cars and airplanes?

The car construction starts just like the knight's horse did—with a cardboard box and some heavy-duty suspenders. Attach the suspenders to a cardboard box and begin to build. Add scored cardboard and poster board for fenders, bumpers, grill, etc. Glue the pieces together and apply mâché to strengthen the form. Build it up with urethane foam and add details. Lost hubcaps make great tires.

The box-and-suspenders armature works for lots of things like airplanes, helicopters, boats and more. Artist Laura Matheson created the Red Baron in this biplane fighter using the basic technique of box and suspenders.

Many people have remarked that larger-than-life sculptures such as those described in this chapter are only usable in a town like New Orleans, where parades and festivals like Mardi Gras promote it. You may find, however, that if you use these ideas as a beginning, you will create your own following and things will happen. At one college workshop on foam, the students got so excited that they organized a parade through the town for football homecoming festivities and performed with their whimsical beasts at half-time. Things happen, so, never say never.

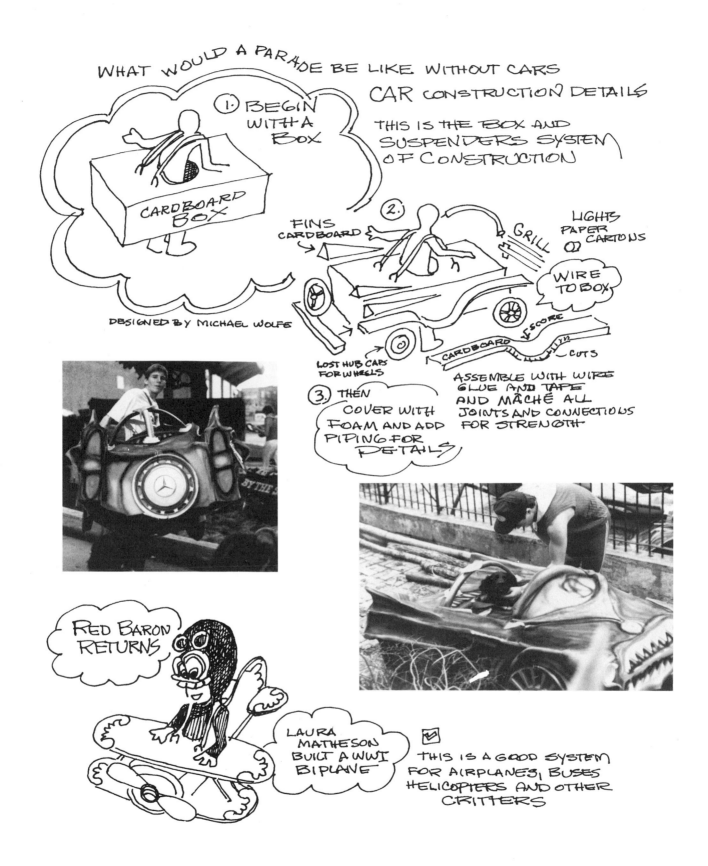

WHAT WOULD A PARADE BE LIKE WITHOUT CARS

CAR CONSTRUCTION DETAILS

THIS IS THE BOX AND SUSPENDERS SYSTEM OF CONSTRUCTION

1. BEGIN WITH A BOX

CARDBOARD BOX

DESIGNED BY MICHAEL WOLFE

2.

FINS CARDBOARD

GRILL

LIGHTS PAPER CARTONS

WIRE TO BOX

LOST HUB CAPS FOR WHEELS

CARDBOARD — SCORE — CUTS

ASSEMBLE WITH WIRE GLUE AND TAPE AND MÂCHÉ ALL JOINTS AND CONNECTIONS FOR STRENGTH

3. THEN COVER WITH FOAM AND ADD PIPING FOR DETAILS

RED BARON RETURNS

LAURA MATHESON BUILT A WWI BIPLANE

☑ THIS IS A GOOD SYSTEM FOR AIRPLANES, BUSES HELICOPTERS AND OTHER CRITTERS

Sources for Materials
Bibliography
Glossary
Index

Sources for Materials

Papier-Mâché

Paper

Corrugated, Kraft paper	Commercial paper companies
Newspaper, Newsprint	Recycle, art supply store or ends of rolls from newspaper company

Adhesives

Wheat paste, methylcellulose, Carpenter's glue	Hardware supply
Flour, laundry starch	Grocery store
Barthform Modeling Emulsion (a water-soluble pressure-sensitive emulsion that is an effective adhesive for contact mâché)	Barthform 4346 Poche Court West New Orleans, LA
Ross art paste (methylcellulose) White glue Instant papier-mâché	Art supply store
3M #30 NF Contact Cement	3M Company 1-800-362-3456 for dealers in your area
Elmer's SAF-T Contact Cement	Hardware supply, school supply, or call Borden Chemical Company 1-800-848-9400

Plaster

Plaster

Moulding plaster Plaster of paris	U. S. Gypsum Company or hardware supply
Other types of plaster	U. S. Gypsum Company 1-800-621-9627

Alginate

Getz Prosthetic Grade Cream	Teledyne Getz Company 1550 Greenleaf Avenue Elk Grove Village, IL 60007 1-800-473-6557

Plaster gauze

Plaster cast	Art supply store
Plaster gauze (wide)	Johnson & Johnson or local medical supply store

Separators

Petroleum jelly   Grocery store, pharmacy

Crisco   Grocery store

Foam

Urethane foam

Urethane foam (padding)   Wholesale carpet company

3/8" or 1/2" inexpensive pieces Carpet store
(not rebow)

Adhesives

3M #74 Foam Fast Adhesive Industrial, contractor or
                               commercial divisions
                               3M Company
                               1-800-362-3456 for dealers in
                               your area

Aleene's Thick Designer   Art supply store
Tacky Glue

Hot melt glue gun and glue Hardware store

Low temp glue gun and glue Craft and sewing stores or
                                department stores

Finish

Air brush inks   Art supply store

Emulsifier for acrylics   Floetrol, latex paint
                               conditioner or
                               The Flood Company
                               P. O. Box 399
                               Hudson, OH 44236

Refillable aerosol spray can Harbor Freight Tools
                                  349 Mission Oaks Boulevard
                                  Camarillo, CA 93011-6010
                                  1-800-423-2567

Styrofoam

Blocks, insulation sheets Builder's supply store

Packaging   Recycle old throw aways

Adhesives

Elmer's SAF-T Contact Cement Hardware supply, school supply
                                  or call
                                  Borden Chemical Company
                                  1-800-848-9400

Tools

Styrofoam cutter   United Art Supply Co., Inc.
                               Box 9219
                               Fort Wayne, IN 46899-9219
                               1-800-322-3247 or
                               Triarco Arts & Crafts
                               14650 28th Avenue, N
                               Plymouth, MN 55447
                               1-800-328-3360

Stanley Surform tools   Hardware supply

Dryvit Primus Adhesive   Dryvit Systems, Inc.
Dryvit Top Coat   One Energy Way
Fiberglass mesh   P. O. Box 1014
                               West Warwick, RI 02893
                               1-800-556-7752

Bibliography

Bush, Martin H. *Sculpture by Duane Hanson*. Wichita: Wichita State University, 1985.

Comins, Jeremy. *Slotted Sculpture from Cardboard*. New York: Lothrop, 1977.

Flower, Cedric, and Alan Fortney. *Puppets: Methods and Materials*. Worcester, Massachusetts: Davis Publications, Inc., 1983.

Grater, Michael. *Make It in Paper*. New York: Dover, 1961.

———. *Paper Maskmaking*. New York: Dover, 1967.

Grooms, Red. *Ruckus Rodeo*. New York: Harry N. Abrams, 1988.

Kenny, Carla, and John B. Kenny. *Design in Papier-Mâché*. Philadelphia: Chilton, 1971.

Merlach, Dona Z. *Creating with Plaster*. Chicago: Reilly and Lee, 1966.

Newman, Thelma Jay Lee. *Paper as an Art and Craft*. New York: Crown, 1973.

Reeder, Dan. *The Simple Screamer*. Salt Lake City: Gill Smith, 1984.

Sivin, Carol. *Maskmaking*. Worcester, Massachusetts: Davis Publications, Inc., 1986.

Shalit, Willa. *Life Cast, Behind the Mask*. Hillsboro, Oregon: Beyond Words, 1992.

Tully, Judd. *Red Grooms and Ruckus Manhattan*. New York: George Braziller, 1977.

Glossary

acrylic   A polymer-based (plastic) paint.

alginate   A seaweed extract used in life casting to create a mold.

armature   The framework or backbone of a piece of sculpture.

assemblage   A three-dimensional work of art, either free-standing or mounted, consisting of many pieces assembled together.

binder   A substance that holds a mixture together.

biomorphic   Abstract forms influenced by nature.

carving   A substractive process of cutting and shaping to create forms.

casting   The reproduction of a model from a mold.

composition   The arrangement of elements in a work of art.

concave   To curve in.

conceptual exercise   An exercise intended to help formulate ideas before starting a work of art.

construction   An additive type of sculpture in which parts are assembled and adhered.

contact glue   A glue that adheres on contact only when both surfaces to which the glue has been applied are dried.

contact method   A method of building sculpture in paper or cardboard coated with contact cement.

contour drawing   A continuous line drawing that conforms to the shapes of the subject.

corrugated paper   A paper having grooves and ridges.

design   The plan used to arrange elements for the purpose of expressing a concept.

design concept   A statement that describes your idea in concrete terms.

Dryvit   A trade name for a system of acrylic products used for very hard exterior surface finishes in the construction industry.

fiberglass mesh   Fabric made of fine glass filaments to reinforce sculpture.

foam (urethane)   A cellular foam fabric usually used as padding under inexpensive carpets.

foam core board   A paper board with foam core.

focal   Center of interest.

form   The content of a work of art as the product of an artist's design, composition and use of materials.

found objects   A loose term for objects not made by the artist but included in the artwork.

free form   Amorphous curvilinear shapes or forms in sculpture usually conceived intuitively.

geometric   Precise shapes or forms that can be defined by lines, planes and solids.

gesture drawing   A quick drawing which emphasizes the pose of the model.

high relief   A sculpture in which areas project at least half of their circumference from the flat surface.

hot melt glue   A high temperature glue dispensed from a glue gun.

kinesthetic   Movement.

kraft paper   Inexpensive brown paper commonly used for paper bags.

laminate   A method of constructing an object in thin layers.

latex   A rubber-based paint.

life casting   The art of casting directly from the human figure.

lift   A positive mold or reproduction of an existing form using papier-mâché.

low melt glue   A glue that melts at a low temperature.

low (bas) relief   A sculpture in which areas project slightly from the flat surface.

media   Material used to create a work of art.

methylcellulose   A type of wallpaper paste used in papier-mâché.

milk coat   A thin preliminary coat of plaster used to fill hard-to-get surfaces in a mold or cast.

mixed media   Use of more than one material in a work of art.

mobile   Sculpture in which shapes are balanced and suspended to allow freedom of movement by air currents.

model   The form from which a mold is made.

modeling paste   A thick acrylic medium used to build up texture.

modular   A sculpture or architectural form composed of a series of modules.

modulate   To manipulate space.

negative mold   A hollow container used to make a cast.

newsprint   A cheap paper used primarily for newspapers.

origami   Japanese paper folding.

paint thinner   Mineral spirits used as a solvent for oil-based paints.

papier-mâché   A French term for mashed paper; a method of making objects from pulp or laminated paper strips soaked in paste.

patina   A simulated metallic finish used to enhance the aesthetic value of sculpture.

piece mold   A mold composed of different sections.

plaster   A white powder produced by heating gypsum. In sculpture plaster is used for molding, casting in direct carving or modeling on an armature.

plaster gauze   A plaster-impregnated gauze used in sculpture.

plaster trap   A sink trap installed to collect plaster residue while allowing water to drain.

plasticene   A nondrying modeling clay.

polyurethane   A plastic varnish.

portland cement   A kind of cement used in concrete.

positive mold   A model duplicated by casting in papier-mâché or plaster.

proportion   The comparative relationship between things or of one part to the whole.

pulp method   A method of papier-mâché for which paper pulp and glue are materials.

rough-in   To cut the general shape in preparation for carving sculpture.

scale   The relative size of a work of art.

scoring   A technique of scratching a line through the outer surface of hard paper or cardboard.

sculpted (scored) paper   Paper sculpture made by scoring and bending paper to create form.

sculpture in the round   A sculpture that can be viewed from all sides.

separator   A substance applied to a mold before casting that aids removal of the cast form the mold.

shellac   An alcohol-based sealer.

shims   Strips placed between sections of a mold which allow the sections to be separated when casting is complete.

solvent   A chemical that will dissolve a substance.

strip method   A method of papier-mâché for which strips of paper soaked in glue are materials.

Styrofoam   An expanded rigid polystyrene plastic.

Styrofoam cutter   A low voltage cutter for Styrofoam.

technical theater   The nonacting components of theater: scenery, props, costumes, lighting.

template   A silhouette of cardboard or thin plywood used as an armature.

texture   The tactile quality of an object.

undercut   A cut made below another to produce an overhang.

wheat paste   Commercial term for wallpaper paste used in papier-mâché.

white glue   Polyvinyl acetate (PVA) glue commonly known in schools as paste.

Index